real decorating for real people™

MATT&SHARI
real decorating for real people™

By Shari Hiller and Matt Fox

Contents

About
Matt & Shari

Shari Hiller was working at Dutch Boy Paints developing color systems. Although she loved her job, the frequent travel took her away from her husband and five-year-old daughter back home in Cleveland. One day she had an idea that would change her life.

"I remember taking a minute to unwind in the family room," Shari says. "Suddenly it occurred to me that wouldn't it be great to videotape my seminars and just send them out to meetings or sell them as instructor videos or even put them on television."

Shari thought about the idea constantly. She envisioned a program that would take viewers through the entire process of redecorating a single room from beginning to end. Soon after, she met Matt Fox, a paint sales representative. She shared her idea with Matt. He, too, caught the vision, and together they refined the concept—real people, real rooms, real decorating. Shari and Matt wrote the script for a nine-minute pilot they called *Home Style*, and then shot it in three days as they redecorated the living room in Shari's brother's bungalow.

With the pilot shot, they excitedly prepared for its screening. They invited ten Dutch Boy executives and drew up a business plan. Matt's mother and Shari cross-stitched *Home Style* logos onto the fronts

of t-shirts for the invitees. Only one executive showed up, but he liked what he saw and agreed to fund the show. It was then renamed *The Look of Home* and debuted in December 1992 as a one-hour, live call-in studio show on the local cable-access channel. From 1992–1993, the decorating duo filmed eighteen episodes of *The Look of Home.* The show was doing well, but Shari and Matt were working overtime.

Then one day, Matt showed Shari an article from *The Wall Street Journal* about a new twenty-four-hour cable network that was about to go on the air. They sent their nine-minute pilot to Kenneth Lowe, HGTV founder and now president-CEO of E.W. Scripps Company. He loved it. HGTV went on the air the morning of December 30, 1994, and the first show broadcast was *Room by Room*. It was an immediate success. Just three years after coming up with the idea, the thirty-minute show that documented the decorative process in a real room in a real house for real people was being aired across the country and beyond.

Today, *Room by Room* is broadcast by HGTV in more than eighty-five million homes worldwide. The show has become an HGTV mainstay, one of the most popular and longest-running home shows on any network. Matt and Shari's online chats draw thousands to the HGTV Web site HGTV.com.

How We Decorate

What better way to get started on your next decorating project than with us right by your side? We wish we could do that, but instead we're bringing you the next best thing. The pages that follow will take you step by step through the same creative process that we use each day.

Getting Started

* **Research**
  - Magazines
  - TV
  - Model homes
  - Internet

* **Budget**

* **Function**
  - Inventory
  - Activities list
  - Evaluate furniture
  - Focal point
  - Floor plan
  - Traffic flow
  - Furniture arrangement
  - Lighting

Shari: Congratulations! You are thinking about trying your hand at decorating. You are about to learn a little bit about yourself, your family and how you live, as well as have fun. Whether you have previously decorated a room before or this is your first attempt, be sure to keep two very important things in mind as you follow our decorative process.

First, if you are not enjoying yourself, stop and re-evaluate, because decorating should be fun. Second, do not let anyone steer you away from something you have fallen in love with, because the goal of decorating is to fall in love with your home all over again.

Here is what you need to do to get the process underway. Start by getting comfortable. Find a quiet place where you can let your mind wander and dream about the beautiful rooms you are about to create. Then read the decorating section of this book so that you have an idea of how the process works. Keep in mind that the process outlined here is written in a linear form. In other words, at first glance the decorating process may seem to be one step after another. However, real decorating does not always happen that way. Some steps will overlap and others may occur out of the order that we present in these pages. Whichever way it happens is fine, as long as the result thrills you.

REALITY CHECK
Matt: I do not have a degree in interior design, but I do have a whole lot of common sense. Now and then you'll find that you need to step out of the decorating dream world and think about decorating for real people the way real people actually do it. So, watch for the Reality Checks. I'll be helping you balance the dream with reality!

Research can be fun

Shari: Research encompasses all kinds of things when it comes to decorating. No matter what room you are working on, make time to check out new ideas and explore your options. It's 100 percent fun and always energizing. Here are some of the things that Matt and I do to get ideas.

Tear apart magazines

This is one of my favorite methods of research, and I believe it to be one of the most eye-opening of all. The process is simple. Just get yourself back into that quiet, cozy place where you can let your mind run free.

Browsing through favorite catalogs and magazines is one of the best ways I know to discover personal style likes and dislikes. When I am working on my own home, this is always my first step.

Begin by paging through some of your favorites. Every time you see something that catches your eye, rip it out. If you usually save all your

magazines, this might be hard to do at first, but it's worth it to accomplish your goal. Do not try to analyze why you like certain things—just keep leafing through the pages, tearing out what you like.

Then set aside the tattered and torn magazines and catalogs and concentrate on the pile of pictures. Now take a good look at each and every one of them.

Is there a common thread running throughout? Can you determine the reason you selected them? Are all of the rooms painted in pastels? Are floral fabrics always used? Do all the rooms seem clean-lined and contemporary? You may even find a room you would like to copy!

Watch decorating and design shows on television!

We would be crazy not to mention the very medium that brought us to you to get decorating ideas galore. Keep watching the wonderful television shows that are available today on many networks, including HGTV.

Visit model homes

I really enjoy this research technique. Many model-home builders hire interior designers to give their homes a polished look. This is a great way to see what designers are doing and what they think is trendy. I want to be aware of new styles and colors in decorating (even all those decorating fads that come and go in a season), and so should you.

If you find you feel comfortable with a particular designer's style, pick up a business card. The designer may be able to help you find one-of-a-kind pieces or even give your design a jump-start for a consultation fee.

mattandshari.com

Take a camera with you and shoot photos of your favorite rooms. The photos will help jog your memory about what you found interesting. Use a notepad to jot ideas and draw sketches.

Surf the Internet

The Internet has become a big part of the world of decorating and design. Just about everyone has a Web site, and there are lots of great ideas and products out there to use as inspiration. (My two recommendations for good, solid decorating advice are mattandshari.com and HGTV.com.)

When your research is complete gather all of the torn-out magazine photos, snapshots of model homes, sketches and anything else that will serve as a guide to your room's new style. Keep everything at your fingertips by inserting all of it into a notebook or binder. This way, you can take it with you as you shop for just the right wallpaper, fabric or accessory!

Set a reasonable budget
REALITY CHECK
Matt: I didn't think Shari was going to let me get a word in edgewise!

What I have to say here is necessary (and I know that whoever is footing the bill will agree with me). BUDGET is important. However, you need to be informed to set a reasonable and realistic budget.

Shari and I decorate for what I call real people—folks who are like us. We are families—hardworking people who want to come home to a place that reflects our personal tastes, makes us feel comfortable and gives us a feeling of pride. We can't afford to spend thousands of dollars on home decorating.

Think about how much you spent at the grocery store last week. Was it $100, $200? And what did you get? How many full bags did you put into the back of your car? Keeping that scenario in mind, how much would you expect to pay to add some new furniture to a room, add paint or wallpaper, perhaps replace the window coverings, and bring in a new piece of art and some pillows? I'm sure you want everything to last at least five years, right? The figure I have in mind has a number and three zeros after it. That's probably more than you thought at first, but now those four-digit numbers seem to make some sense, don't they?

As Shari always says, "Create your dream plan, and then work at it in baby steps!" **There's nothing wrong with a multiyear design plan.**

Form follows function

Shari: What does that really mean? Form follows function. My husband reminds me of this all the time. It means you should make sure the room is functioning for you and your family first, and then create the form, or the decorative part. I hate to admit it, but he's right. You won't be happy in the long run with a beautiful room that doesn't function for you. Do the hard part first and create a room that functions for your needs. The fun will follow!

Take inventory. Every room has something that you need to consider while you are decorating. It could be a carpet color, cathedral ceiling or certain furniture pieces that must stay. Take some time to jot down these special needs so they are fresh in your mind as you get started. These challenges can be overcome if you research your options. For instance, are there hardwood floors under the less-than-perfect carpet? Could the cathedral ceiling be highlighted with color? Would painting the odd furniture pieces help them work in the room? Like it or not, we seldom start from scratch, and these challenges can be the start of something really wonderful!

REALITY CHECK
Matt: This is a good time to look over the walls, ceilings and floors of your room in great detail. Check for cracks that need to be filled, trim that needs repair, vents that should be vacuumed and carpeting that needs a professional cleaning. This is the time to get all of those repairs and special cleaning jobs out of the way, before the new furniture is delivered or new paint and wallpaper are installed. For some great preparation tips, check pages 18-25!

Shari: Make an activities list. As exciting as it is to get started with the decorative process, it is very important to make sure that your room is functioning. When we talk about function, we mean, "Can you use your furnished room to its fullest potential?" Are there additional functions you would like to include in the redesign of your room that you had not previously thought about?

The best way to figure this out is to make an *activities* list of everything you do in the room, along with any other uses that you might want to include.

Next, create a *needs* list. Jot down all furniture, storage or lighting requirements for the activities that you listed. Go crazy with your wish list and include everything you can think of. Creative thinking at this point will mean that you will be more likely to meet and exceed your expectations for the room.

After you have finished itemizing your needs, make an *inventory* list of the items you already have. Sometimes you

Activities	Needs
Watching TV	TV entertainment center
Naps	Comfortable sofa
Sewing projects	Table, storage & good lighting
Homework	

Inventory	Shopping List
TV	Entertainment center
Sofa	Table, storage & good lighting

will discover that a room is in better shape than you first thought.

Then make a *shopping* list of the items necessary to fulfill all of the room's needs.

Evaluate the current furniture. Now comes the time to be ruthless. Take each of the items on your inventory list, beginning with the furniture, and determine whether it is appropriate for the activities in the room. If a piece of furniture isn't

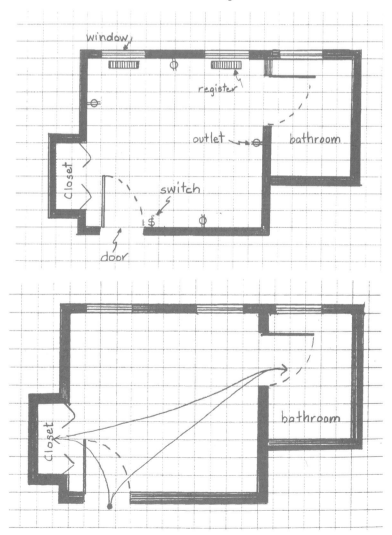

working, or if it is too large or too small for the size of the room, get rid of it, or trade it for something else around the house that may be more appropriate. This is a great time to do some swapping with friends and family. It doesn't cost a thing, and everyone gets a little change.

If there are no other options and you really do need a new piece, add it to the shopping list, including color options and style options as well. You may have a clipping from your research that has just the piece you need to finish off the room.

Find a focal point. A focal point is either the first thing you see when you enter a room, or it is the item you decide you want everyone to see when entering your room. A natural focal point is a fireplace or an entertainment center. In a bedroom, it should be the bed. If your room doesn't have a natural focal point, you can create one with a dramatic area rug, a well-lit piece of art or just a fabulous outdoor view. Some rooms have several focal points. You may need to determine if, for example, the fireplace is the winter focal point and the view is the summer focal point.

Think about your room. Does it have a natural focal point that you can highlight, or do you need to create one?

Knowing your room's focal point will help you with floor planning, our next step in real decorating.

Create a floor plan. A floor plan of your room will help you place furniture in a workable arrangement. This will also show you areas that might need additional pieces. Grab a tape measure, a pencil and a piece of paper and get busy measuring the space. Make sure to measure and mark the placement of outlets, switches and registers, not to mention doors and windows.

After you have all the measurements, create a floor plan to scale on one-quarter-inch graph paper. The scale drawing allows you to use furniture pieces also drawn to scale and move them around the room without using a single back muscle!

There are standard guidelines for creating floor plans. On one-quarter-inch graph paper, one square equals one foot, so if you need to indicate a ten-foot wall, draw along one of the lines for ten squares. Interior walls are generally four to six inches thick, so those lines should be a half square in thickness. Windows are outlined but left open with small glass panes drawn in the center, and doorways are left completely open with doors drawn perpendicular to the wall at the hinged corner.

Traffic flow. After you have completed the floor plan, consider the traffic flow of the room without the furniture. To do this, lightly pencil in the path you would take through the room to get from one doorway to another, or the direct path to the closet or adjacent bathroom. These light pencil lines will help you determine where not to place furniture for the best traffic flow through the room.

Furniture arrangement. To create a furniture layout, you must measure all of the furniture that will stay in the room. You will see the furniture on the floor plan by its width and depth. One of the easiest ways to get your arrangement started is with furniture cutouts drawn to the same scale as the floor plan, where one foot on the furniture equals one-quarter-inch. As a rule, direct the main furniture pieces toward the focal point, keeping major traffic patterns open. After you have those in place, fill in with the other items that you have available, leaving spaces for pieces yet to come. Be sure to balance high and low as well as heavy and light pieces around the room.

REALITY CHECK
Matt: Before continuing on with lighting and the whole decorating process,

I recommend that you set up your room in the arrangement you have just created, and then live with it for a while to be sure this is the best arrangement for you and your family. If it isn't, then reconsider some of the new pieces you are planning to purchase. By the way, here's a furniture-moving tip: Get a few of those plastic-based moving glides at your local home-center store. Those glides are the best thing that ever happened in the decorating world ... and my back couldn't agree more!

Shari: **Lighting.** Lighting is extremely important to every decorating project. It should be selected for the functions of the room as well as for visual appeal. Every task will require either direct lighting from a lamp for reading or studying or indirect lights that simply brighten the room for conversation or TV viewing. Accent lighting, such as floor spots, track lighting or recessed spots, is a wonderful addition to any room. You can spotlight a favorite piece of art, send glorious shadows to the ceiling through a leafy plant or even just graze the surface of a rich brick fireplace.

Look over the arrangement of furniture you have developed.

Is it possible to bring light to all the tasks you have incorporated? Can new lighting be added to the ceiling in the form of track or recessed fixtures? Even a pendant lamp can be hung anywhere on a ceiling and attractively plugged into a wall outlet if that is your only option.

When you go through all the planning it takes to create a truly work-able, livable space, you have taken the time to really design the room. When you add pillows and accessories here and there, you are deco-rating, not designing. Only after you have a well-planned and well-designed room is it time to start the decorating!

Creating the mood
What we really mean when we talk about decorating a room

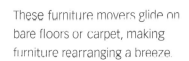

These furniture movers glide on bare floors or carpet, making furniture rearranging a breeze.

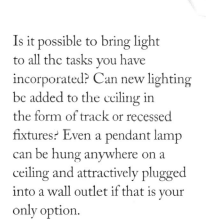

Rearranging furniture on a scaled floor plan is easy with paper furniture cutouts.

is using color, pattern and texture along with style, shape and art objects to create a mood or feeling in a space. There is a lot to think about during this phase of decorating a room.

Review your research notes and sketches and pull out the photos that first piqued your interest. Discover all over again what it was about the photos that made you tear them out or save them. This will help as you move ahead with the challenging but fun process of decorating your room.

REALITY CHECK

Matt: As cool as the finished room is going to be, once it's done, all the fun is over. Enjoy the process and don't rush. The room isn't going anywhere and, as each new item or project is added, it will take on a new feel, have new dimensions and provide new things to think about. Decorating is a blast, and I for one want it to last as long as possible!

Shari: Get inspired. By far, the easiest way to get started with a complicated decorating project is to first select an inspiration piece. In a bedroom, it could be

a comforter full of colors and patterns that make you smile. For a kitchen, try a wallpaper border or dinnerware pattern to get the creative juices flowing.

A piece of art, an area rug, a collection, a scarf— anything with color and pattern can be inspirational. It has to be a great color and style guide, helping you to visualize a room designed around it. Most of all, if you love it—absolutely love it—you'll end up feeling the same way about your finished room.

Select a theme name. After you have selected an inspiration piece, take note of everything you like about it— from color to pattern to what it represents to you. If you then give your inspiration a theme name, such as "Spring Garden," it will make decisions for the decor of the room much easier. The more specific the theme name, as in "Traditional Midwest Spring Garden," the easier the decorating will be.

For example, think about a traditional Midwest spring garden and what that conjures up in your mind. For me it's the spring flowers of daffodils, hyacinths, tulips and crocuses, rain and umbrellas, robins and nests. Easter can slide in there if I let it with wonderful

pastels and baskets. For me, this is when the room starts to develop. I see soft blue walls with a linen texture, linen-colored upholstery and great pastel pillows. The wood furniture seems like it should be white or at least light with either a cottage look or a contemporary feel. Forced bulbs, great spring-colored prints and sheers on the windows with a spring-patterned window topper finish off the look.

This is what I'm talking about when I say an inspiration piece and a theme name can make your decorating decisions so much easier!

REALITY CHECK

Matt: Be sure that this new, wonderful inspiration piece blends well with the rest of your home. For example, you don't want three rooms that open to each other to be vastly different in theme, color or style.

Shari: Hue, chroma, color. Hmmm, where to begin. Without an inspiration piece, this section about color would have to be extremely long and involved. However, since you have the colors and palette of the inspiration piece to use as a guide, this section will be shorter.

To begin, it works best to choose three colors for a

room—a dominant color, a secondary color and an accent.

The dominant color could be the dominant color of your inspiration piece. It is a color that you could use for the walls, floor and fabric backgrounds. Usually, it is not the brightest color in the palette, but a more neutral one. This is not to say that all rooms have to be done in neutrals, but it is a safe route to go if you are unsure of your skill in selecting color. If you prefer, your wall color could be an accent color, but the majority of the furnishings might have to be toned down so the accent can be just that.

The secondary color is found throughout the room in fabrics, patterns and accessories.

The accent color is usually used sparingly to give energy or excitement to a room.

If your patterns have more than three colors, take a few minutes to analyze the pattern. You may have to stand back and ask a few questions. Which is the dominant color? Which is secondary? Which one really adds punch to the fabric? Then consider how and where you will use those three main colors in the room.

REALITY CHECK

the best way to decide what color to put on the walls, and even the furniture, is to paint sample boards. You can make them quickly and easily out of the sides of a cardboard box. Paint them, tape them up on the wall, or place them over the sofa. Look at them at various times during the day and night in all lighting conditions. Move them around the room until you are satisfied that you love the colors!

Shari: **Pattern.** Mixing patterns is definitely an art. However, many manufacturers are now mixing them, so you can see them together before you purchase. Entire living room suites are available already well blended. If you are selecting fabrics, many fabric stores show fabrics that mix and match next to each other on the fabric rack. It is easier than ever before to combine stripes with florals and checks with paisleys! Keep in mind a few rules when selecting several patterns.

First, keep the background color the same throughout. It is difficult to combine a white background floral with a cream and color stripe.

Second, make sure that all of the patterns share the same groups of colors, not

necessarily the same number of colors.

Third, vary the scale of the print. A large floral works better with a medium check than a large check. Your goal is to create harmony among the patterns, not a fight for dominance.

Texture. You can easily understand the need for texture when you enter an undecorated bathroom. The cold smooth tile mixed with the smooth laminate counter top and all that shiny porcelain doesn't say warm and cozy to me! However, the addition of terry-cloth towels, fuzzy area rugs, a fabric shower curtain and window coverings turn cold to cozy through the use of texture. Sometimes texture is an illusion, as in faux painting techniques or printed laminates or even granite surfaces. It's there, but you can't really feel it. Even those textures can add interest and warm up a space. Just remember that too much of one texture can become tiresome. Use a variety to keep the room interesting, or alter the texture in the room for the seasons.

Furniture—again. You are on a roll now. The room is functioning well, and you've selected the colors and patterns to suit your taste. You even have an idea for just the right amount of texture

to make everyone in your family happy. Before you start painting and buying new pieces, evaluate your present furniture one more time. You already know your current pieces function well. Now that you've spent all that time developing the color palette to go with your inspiration piece and the right combination of pattern and texture, are those original pieces of furniture still right? Are they in the best colors, patterns and textures to fit the new look you are creating for your room?

If not, then put your foot down, add the item to your shopping list and stick with the dream. Remember, this project may take a year or two to finish, and that's fine when you have a plan in place.

REALITY CHECK

Matt: Snap out of the decorating dream for a moment. Is there a way to use the furniture you already have and still make the dream a reality? Re-upholstering or even slipcovers are great options. Shari makes them all the time. Stop and think about those pieces that don't match the new room. I have painted many cabinets and tables with much success. Distressing techniques and

faux finishes allow you to alter a piece of furniture to look like just about anything. Is there something that could be done to fix them up? If you exhaust all of these options, visit garage sales or secondhand shops to find items that can be altered to fit your needs.

Shari: Three layers of interest. Before all the work begins, be sure to double-check your plans. One idea that works for me is to imagine all the changes I plan to make to the room. If I have done my homework and collected swatches and drawn sketches, I have a good idea what the finished room will look like. I think about the room as if it is sliced horizontally into three layers: the top third of the room, the middle third and the bottom third. Then I consider what I have planned for each level. Are there items of interest in every level? If I have placed only low furniture in the room, I will need to compensate with a special window treatment that has an interesting topper.

Try to put something at every level that catches your eye. The more slowly you take in the beauty of a room, the more interesting it becomes.

Putting it all together

Up to this point, you should be doing your research, drawing up floor plans, planning a budget, and collecting swatches and samples of fabric, paint, carpet and wallpaper you would like to use in your dream room. But there does come a time when you actually have to start doing the projects. Well, that time has arrived. Order items that have long lead times, get the sewing machine out and make those slipcovers and window coverings, and sweep up the shop and get started on those shelves!

If you are looking for project ideas and instructions for this step in the decorative process, check out our Web site, mattandshari.com, for an ever-increasing list of every type of project imaginable. And don't forget what we stated early on—have fun and enjoy the process. This is what decorating is all about!

The STUFF

What do I mean by "stuff"? The "stuff" is all the accessories. "Stuff" is my personal tribute to Matt. He loves to give me a hard time about how much "stuff" I bring into a room before I make my final decisions.

Actually, I should start with congratulations! Isn't it a great feeling to have the projects complete? However, the room still needs something.

Accessories are the personal touches that turn a well-planned room into a home. They are also the vase you bought on vacation and the framed family photos that warm your heart. An accessory could be a pillow made by your grandmother, or it could be something brand-new that perfectly fits your theme and makes you giddy when you enter your new room!

Generally, accessories should support your theme. Signed, framed pictures of football stars may be your favorite collectible, but how will they look in your "Traditional Midwest Spring Garden" theme? Pretty bad, I would guess. However, give yourself a little leeway here. A collection of antique spoons may not tie directly to gardening, but they might be just the personal touch that makes your room feel like you!

Balance in all zones

Last, but not least, when you think the room is finished, do a final check. This is one of my favorite parts of the process. It's your opportunity to evaluate what you've done and make any adjustments. I stand and sit in all different places of the room—places I think will be used often—and

take in the view. This is how I can tell if I have too much of one color on one side of the room and not enough on the other, or if I'm missing an accessory on a table or shelf. I use this time to gently adjust the arrangement of lamps and accessories or nudge a table over an inch.

These are the final tweaks that are tremendously satisfying. Once everything is in just the right place, you'll find that you can't stop looking at the room you created. Your family will be pulled to it as well, and your friends will say things that make you feel proud—as well you should be. This is quite an accomplishment. Rooms don't just fall together. It takes planning, persistence and a lot of time and effort.

Celebrate! Quick! Before you start thinking about redecorating the next room!

REALITY CHECK

Matt: The reality of the situation is that you've probably already started the next room, because this decorating stuff is habit-forming. But that's all right. It's a joyous journey of learning, trying and overcoming the odds. All you need to do now is pass on the joy by getting someone else started!

How-To Basics
Preparing a Room

The key to any good design is the preparation at the start of the process. One of the keys to doing the job correctly and in a timely fashion is to follow the same steps for every room. Before we even begin, we make sure that we have all the tools and materials that we need for any given project.

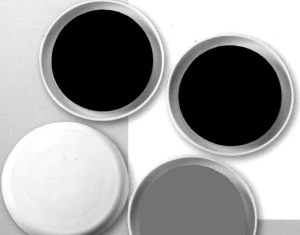

Reserve an area near the room you will be working on to set up a "shop." This is where everything you need, from paint brushes to ladders, will be stored. The less running back and forth to the garage or the store, the less time the prep work will take. Following these steps will make the process go smoothly and add to the overall satisfaction of a well-designed room.

1 **Eliminate the clutter.** If you haven't used something in a year—get rid of it! One of the biggest obstacles when working on a room is having too much stuff. Look around the room. Do you really need that stack of old magazines? If you haven't looked at them in more than six months, donate them to a library or a school. If a worn-out chair has seen better days, get rid of it. This is the time to keep only what you really need. It's hard, but it needs to be done.

2 **After you have removed unwanted items,** start removing anything in the room that can get broken during the preparation process. Purchase several plastic bins that can hold all the items safely (laundry baskets work great for this). The more things you can remove from the room, the easier it will be to get things done. Place all the items in an adjacent room out of the way of the work path.

3 **Move all furniture** to the center of the room. If you don't have someone who can help you, purchase a set of furniture glides. They slip beneath the legs of the furniture, and the plastic bottoms make it possible for one person to maneuver furniture from one end of the room to another. Make sure to leave enough space so you can reach all of the ceiling if it needs to be painted.

4 **Use thin plastic sheets** to cover all the furniture. Most paint stores and home-

center stores sell them. They will protect the furniture from any dust that may be created or paint that may be dripped during the prep and painting process. If need be, use painter's blue tape to keep the plastic from slipping off the furniture.

Place canvas drop cloths on the floor. We use 4 x 12 runners along the edges of the room and larger tarps for the center. If the project will be messy, such as painting, fold the drop cloths in half. If you happen to spill something, the double layer will prevent it from seeping onto the carpet. *Note: It's handy to have a pair of shoes that you wear only for prepping. Then, whenever you leave the room, slip them off to prevent tracking wet paint through other parts of the house.*

5 **Remove any hardware,** such as curtain rods and shelf brackets, from the walls to prevent getting paint on it. If the hardware includes small parts that can easily become lost, place the parts in a zipper bag and mark the bag with a permanent marker so you remember what room it belongs in. If it is an item that is still in good shape but will not be reused,

consider saving it for a garage sale, or donate it to a worthy cause.

As you remove items that will not be replaced from the walls, fill the resulting holes with spackling compound. The spackling compound will dry while you are doing other prep, which means you'll be able to start painting sooner. Most paint stores sell a flush spackling compound, which can be applied flush to the wall, eliminating any sanding. It's great for smaller holes and gaps. If the hole is too large, you may want to consider a sanding spackling or wall mud.

6 **Probably the most time-consuming** and dreaded part of the preparation process is sanding woodwork. If you are

painting the trim in a room, all of it must be sanded in order for the new coat of trim paint to adhere.

Working from the top down, begin by sanding any ceiling trim, such as crown molding. A piece of 220-grit sandpaper folded in thirds makes a convenient sanding pad. Sand all of the trim, working from high to low. The idea is to etch the surface, not to sand down to bare wood, so don't be too aggressive.

7 **After the spackling compound is dry,** sand the surface smooth. If it's a large surface area, rent or purchase a pole sander. It will cut the sanding process down to hardly any time at all.

Tip: Your fingertips make a really neat finish sander. Lightly rub them over any spackling that you have already sanded with paper. Your fingers will give the spackling a finish that can't be beat, leaving no sandpaper marks.

8 **Remove all dust** from every surface. Start by using an old paintbrush to dust down all the walls and trim. Work from the ceiling down, pushing the dust onto the floor tarps. Follow up with a light washing with a clean, damp rag.

Remove the drop cloths and take them outside to shake off the dust. Use a brush attachment to vacuum the walls and trim, and then vacuum the floor. Replace all the drop cloths.

9 **Use a caulking gun** and latex silicone caulk to fill cracks or gaps in the trim and walls. For a large gap, make several applications to prevent shrinkage—don't try to fill it all at once.

10 **Spot-prime all bare wood** and spackling compound. Use a latex wall and wood primer. This will help even out the coverage of the paint. If you have just a small amount of priming to do, use a foam brush that can be stored overnight in aluminum foil for the next day's use or simply thrown away.

Most of the time, the first day of a project is the preparation day. After the spackling, caulking and priming are done, allow everything to dry and cure overnight. The room will be ready to go in the morning, and you will be more rested for the really fun stuff yet to come.

Painting Tools & Tips

Roller tray and plastic liner

Purchase a paint tray into which an inexpensive plastic liner can be inserted. The plastic liner is easier to clean or it can just be thrown away. **Cleanup tip:** *When painting takes more than one day, store the paint tray and roller cover in a sealed plastic garbage bag. The paint will not dry out, and you won't have to clean the tray or roller cover.*

Roller frames

A 9-inch roller frame is standard. Look for quick-release frames that make it easier to remove the roller cover. Just tap the frame against a plastic pail and the roller cover will slide right off.
Roller tip: *Look for roller frames that can be attached to an extension pole. An extension pole makes it much easier to roll paint onto large walls and ceilings. The longer pole gives you more leverage and you will be able to cover a larger area in less time.*

Roller covers

Roller covers are made out of different materials for different types of paint and different nap thicknesses for different wall surfaces. The general rules of thumb are:

- If the nap is natural, such as mohair, it's best for oil-based products. If the nap is man-made, it's best for latex products.
- If the nap is thick, it's for rougher surfaces. Heavily stuccoed walls call for thicker roller covers, with thicknessess of 1 to 1½ inches.
- For a smooth wall, like a bathroom wall with no texture, a ¼-inch nap is the best bet.

For example, if you are painting a semi-smooth living room wall, choose a polyester roller cover that is about ½ inch thick. If in doubt, ask a paint store clerk.

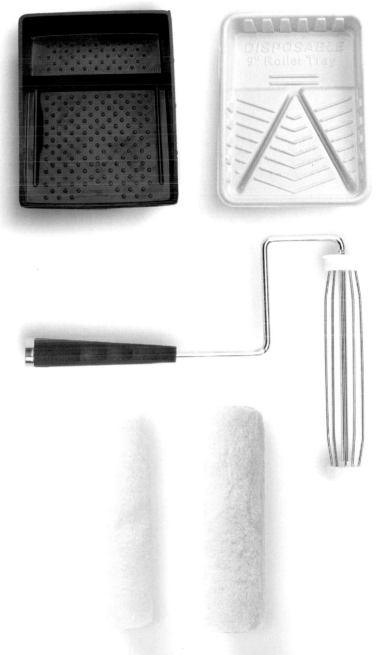

Paint pail

Instead of carrying a full gallon of paint around the room while you paint, pour about an inch into a plastic pail. That way you're not carrying around a lot of weight, and you don't run the risk of spilling a whole gallon of paint on the floor.

Pail tip: *When cleaning the pail after use, pour the paint back in the can, allow the remaining paint to dry in the pail, and then peel it out of the bucket and throw it away. No mess, no wasted water.*

Painter's blue tape

One of the hardest things to do is paint a straight edge. Use painter's blue tape and you will have no problem. This low-tack tape can be left on the trim for several days and then easily removed without pulling and damaging the trim.

Tape tip: *If you have left tape on too long, use a low setting on a hair dryer to warm up the tape adhesive and it will pull away nicely. Clean up any glue residue with a little paint thinner.*

5-in-1 tool

For what it costs, slightly less than eight dollars, this tool is a painter's favorite. You can use this tool as a putty knife, to scrape paint off roller covers, to open up cracks so that you can better fill them with spackling compound—the list of uses goes on and on! Some models can even be used as a hammer, with the blunt end strong enough to drive a nail.

5-in-1 tip: *Use the 5-in-1 to open paint cans. It sure beats ruining the tip of a good screwdriver.*

Paper towels and clean rags

Keep a generous supply handy. Need we say more?

Flexible putty knife

Use this handy tool to apply spackling compound—the better the flex, the easier to apply.

Caulking gun

Purchase one that has a cutter in the handle to cut off the tip of the tube. It should also have a plunger along the length to puncture the seal of the caulk tube.

Caulking tip: *Don't allow caulk to freeze. Just like latex paint, it will lose its integrity.*

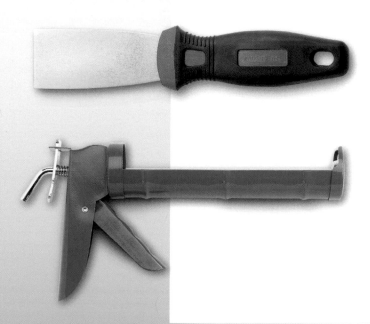

Paintbrushes

A quality paintbrush is the bread-and-butter tool for professional painters. Show me a painter's toolbox and I'll show you a paintbrush that is taken care of like a favorite family pet. Most brushes can last several years when proper care is given to the brush. When you choose a brush, keep these things in mind.

- Natural bristle brushes, like hogs hair and boar bristles, are meant for oil-based paints. They may cost more, but they leave very few or no brush strokes. If they are used for oil-based paints, brushes must be cleaned with paint thinner or mineral spirits.
- Synthetic/polyester bristle brushes are meant for latex paints. They are designed to hold large amounts of paint and have stiffer bristles, but are workhorses for do-it-yourselfers. Clean with soap and water.

The four brushes to have in your paint kit

- 4-inch straight brush, polyester, for dusting walls and trim. This is a must-have.
- 2½-inch tapered brush, polyester, for paint trim and cutting in.
- 2½-inch tapered natural bristle brush for those times where oil-based paint is the only option.
- 2½-inch straight brush, polyester, for cutting in and general painting.

Brush tip: Don't skimp on what you pay for your brushes. If you are a true do-it-yourselfer, you will be using them for a long time. The cheaper the brush, the harder it is to use. Remember, patience and the proper tools are what make a great painter great!

Brush-care basics

Always clean a brush as soon as you are finished painting for the day. If the paint is allowed to dry, it will be harder to clean. At the very least, rinse the brush and place the bristles in water—but only for a short time. Too much water and the glue holding the bristles will start to fail.

- Use a wire brush to remove any dried-on paint. Work down through the bristles, combing down from the handle into the bristles. Be gentle.
- Use a pail to rinse the brush, placing water into the bucket. Work the water into the bristle up into the ferrule (the metal part of the brush). Rinse until the water in the bucket remains clear.
- Spin the brush between the palms of your hands to remove all excess water. Don't let a brush dry without removing most of the water. Without proper care, the glue in the handle will start to fail.
- When you purchase a brush, keep the packaging. Use it to store the brush—the cover will keep the bristles straight and in line. If you lose the packaging, store the brush wrapped in a piece of newspaper.

Matt's Essential Tool Kit

My tool box isn't the traditional type—it's actually a 5-gallon bucket with a tool liner called a Bucket Boss. Open at the top, it has pockets that hold my favorite selection of tools. I like to see everything at once, and this bucket is open enough for me to tell at a glance just what is in it.

Inside the bucket:

- 14.5-volt cordless drill. I always have extra batteries charging at home that I pick up as I walk out the door in the morning.
- 16-oz. claw hammer for nailing and removing nails.
- Japanese handsaw for cutting trim and small pieces of wood. It's the best handsaw I own and comes in many sizes. My toolbox saw is about 12 inches long.
- One or two pairs of pliers. I like the RoboGrip brand by Sears. Most home centers have their own brand—try out several types until you find one or two favorites of your own.
- Two 5-in-1 painter's tools.
- Two types of putty knife: a flex blade for applying spackling compound and a stiff blade for glazing windows and scraping loose paint.
- Stud finder. I can't live without one—it's essential for hanging artwork and shelving units.
- Assorted screwdrivers. I prefer a single driver with bits stored in the handle—all-in-one tool—but I do keep a larger slotted and Phillips head in the bucket for tough jobs. I have recently added a square head driver for driving deck screws.
- Scissors, usually replaced every week because Shari always borrows mine.
- An old paintbrush to use for dusting.

- A set of chisels from ¼ inch to 1½ inches. I keep the blades wrapped in a soft cloth to protect them.
- Chain spreaders, found in most lighting stores for installing fans and chandeliers.
- Box of drill bits. You can't have enough bits. I have a set of bits for metal and one for wood.
- A can of WD-40 for loosening screws and general purposes. It's great for removing stickers from glass.
- Carpenter's square for on-site construction. I also keep a speed square in the bucket to use as a guide for cutting lumber with my circular saw.

Around the outside of the bucket:

- Small torpedo level—a great tool for any type of leveling.
- Carpenter's ruler, the kind that folds like an accordian. What a cool tool; it's the type your granddad would have in his tool box.
- Wire cutters and wire splicer.
- Crescent (adjustable) wrench, in case I have to do a little plumbing.
- Electrical tape in a plastic case for protection.
- Circuit tester, a plug-in model and a wire model. I never do electrical work without one.
- An assortment of spade bits and larger drill bits.
- An awl, which looks like an ice pick. I use this to make pilot holes for drilling and for marking locations for carpentry. It's my second favorite tool.
- Assorted pencils and black markers and, of course, several sharpeners.
- An assortment of nail sets for setting nails.
- Small flashlight, which I use more often than you would think.

Let's Add Power!

There are two unmistakable signs that you're ready to add to your power tool collection. The first sign is when you begin to make more space in your garage or basement for tools. The other is when you contemplate the purchase of a workbench. At the root of these two acts is a growing confidence in your skills as a do-it-yourselfer. The more self-assured you become, the more apt you are to move up to power tools. As your skill develops, so does your desire to tackle more difficult projects. It's only natural to add power tools to your collection.

For those who are making their first foray into power tools, I suggest the following "must-haves" for any tool-toting guy or gal.

Circular Saw

This tool is an essential. It will make fast, straight cuts in wood. If you want to build, this is the tool you'll use most often. Choose a saw with a 7¼-inch blade, which will allow you to cut through two-inch lumber. With a variety of specialty blades you can cut almost anything—wood, metal and even concrete.

Saw tips: Circular saw blades cut as they rotate upward, so the top face of the work piece could splinter. Position the good side of the piece facing down.

Don't be tempted to throw away a dull blade. They can be sharpened!

Cordless Drill

Without a doubt, this is the power tool I reach for most throughout the day. I have a variety of different drills with different voltages for different tasks. I use an 8-volt drill for household tasks, and I have a 14-volt on my workbench for more torque and power.

This is the type of tool you need to test-drive. Most home centers have a station where drills are set up or on display. Try them all. The weight and power of the drill is a personal preference. Most cordless drills have a keyless chuck, which means you can change drill bits in a flash. Look for that feature.

Drill tip: Always buy an extra battery so one can be charging at all times.

Variable Speed Jigsaw

This is the tool to use when you need to cut something with curves. Choose a saw that is rated to cut 2-inch-thick softwood and ¾-inch hardwood stock. Different cutting blades may require different cutting speeds, so make sure you choose a jigsaw with variable speeds.

Jigsaw tips: Coarse-tooth blades need more speed than fine-tooth blades.

Don't force a jigsaw blade into a cut because the blade is likely to break.

Miter Saw

The power miter saw is versatile and portable. This tool is used for finish carpentry like cutting crown molding and other woodworking projects. There are many models to choose from. The one in my shop is a 12-inch sliding compound miter saw. I can cut lumber up to 10 inches wide. I also have a 10-inch saw for smaller projects.

Miter saw tip: The miter saw's cut depends on the blade and the speed of the blade as it is forced into the wood. Make sure the motor has reached full speed before cutting, and lower the saw arm slowly for best results.

Router

I love my router. It makes me look good! I use it to add decorative detail, cut grooves and trim laminate. It is the tool that finishes the cutting.

Router tip: Router bits spin in a clockwise direction, so the tool will drift to the left. For the best control, move the router from left to right so that the cutting edge of the bit feeds into the wood.

Palm Sander

Buy a good quality electric palm sander with a dust collection attachment. This little workhorse will cut down your sanding time by more than half. For convenience, get a palm sander that allows you to affix adhesive-backed sandpaper directly to a rubber pad on the sander.

Sander tip: Just because you have a sander doesn't mean you can skip a step. Always start with a coarse-grit sandpaper (like 100 grit) and move to a finer-grit sandpaper (like 220 grit). A smooth finish depends on the type of sandpaper you use.

I caution you to avoid the temptation of buying tools just for the sake of having them. Often it makes more sense to rent them than to buy them. Purchase tools that help get the job done and that you enjoy using. Always ask yourself, "Do I really need this?" If the answer is "yes," then go ahead, plug in and put it to work!

Outside it's a house. Inside it's a home— full of warmth, personality, inspiration and ideas. Turn the page and come inside …

Entryways

An entryway is the first
opportunity for guests to
learn something about you
and your family. A quick
glance at your entryway
can say more about you than
you could ever imagine.

What's Right?

Architectural Details

The curved staircase and matching curved wall attract attention, making them natural focal points.

Before

This Entryway is huge, and functionally it can handle additional seating and some storage. Aesthetically, it is full of interesting details, from the curved staircase to the softly curving wall. However, these areas of high interest are being ignored. Consider any unique features of your room when you begin decorating. As with this entryway, you may have a diamond in the rough!

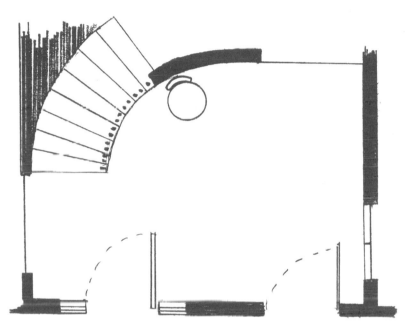

Spacious Floor Plan

An entryway like this is a dream come true for many. Even though this room is broken up with doorways, **plenty of wall space remains for additional storage pieces or displaying artwork.** Best of all, this entryway is large enough to greet guests comfortably and put on coats and outdoor gear.

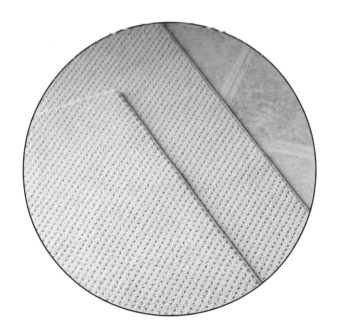

Interesting Rug Configuration

Overlapping rectangular area rugs by the front door give the room a unique look. They function well and their color tone is just right, but does the rectangular shape work with the curved walls? Hmmm …

What's Wrong?

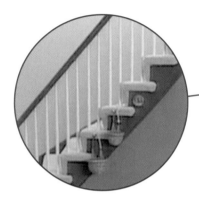

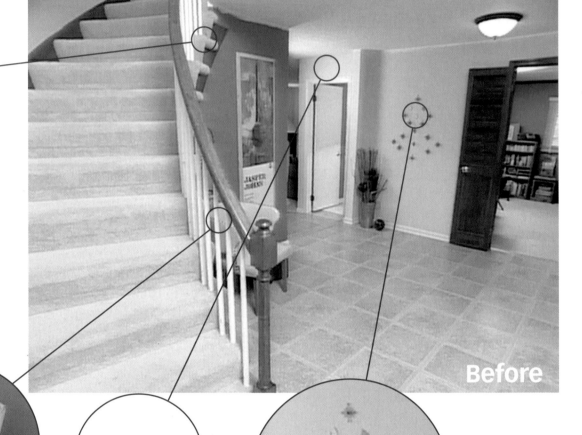

Before

Mixture of Wood Finishes

In this entryway, stained wood trim is mixed with white painted trim. Often, this mix works. Here, the balance of stain to paint isn't right, and the dark stained pieces overpower the white painted areas.

Inadequate Storage

An entryway this size can handle a storage piece or two that can hold school bags, mail, newspapers, rain gear and keys.

No Unifying Color Statement

The entryway is the perfect place to start a home color scheme. This can be done with a colorful area rug, artwork or even a floral arrangement.

Outdated Art and Accessories

If you've used the same accessories for ten years, a change will do you and your room some good.

Let's Get Started!

Since this entryway doesn't function well, a floor plan is a good place to start. When planning, it's necessary to remember that this entryway is like a bus station with people constantly coming and going through the space. The children usually leave instruments and school belongings here, along with the mail, keys, jackets and anything else imaginable. **Start with function by adding storage pieces** to help keep clutter under control.

Find an inspiration piece to get the decorating started. The inspiration piece for this entry is a crewel wall hanging that brings together all the colors the homeowner loves in one very fun geometric design.

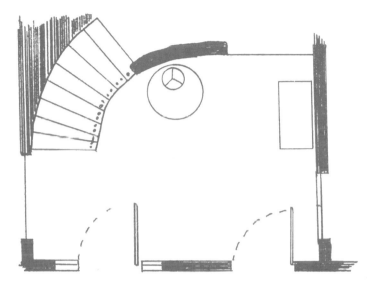

Once an inspiration piece has been chosen, the rest of the choices, from paint and furniture to window coverings, become so much easier. Just select colors and finishes that coordinate with it.

Fixes

No Storage?
Add Cabinetry and Shelves!

A bare five-foot wall provides plenty of space for a storage cabinet and decorative shelves. This cabinet offers enough covered storage for the homeowners' needs. We purchased an unfinished cabinet and painted it black to enhance the black in the inspiration piece.

To complement the cabinet, we installed handmade cantilevered shelves above it, which provide room for baskets in which to place keys and mail, and display space for additional accessories. Remember, this is the first room anyone sees when entering the home, so looks are important!

Mixture of Wood Finishes?
Paint!

When there is a mixture of stained and painted finishes, the most practical solution is to paint everything.

No Unifying Color Statement?
Get Inspired!

An inspiration piece that has a pattern, a collection of colors and a style that speaks to you can be the decorative guide to everything you do in your home. This crewel wall hanging offers plenty of colors to pick up throughout the house and gives the impression that a bold, contemporary style will be found within.

Outdated Art and Accessories?
Time to Buy New!

There are so many options available for accessories today. Many retail stores carry a large variety of decorative items to fit all styles. Don't forget to check out discount stores, antique shops, specialty shops and even garage sales for unique and unexpected additions to your home.

Fixes

Skirted Round Table

A round table highlights the beautiful curved walls in the entryway. Stay within your decorating budget by building one to fit the space. An easy-to-sew round tablecloth covers the table with style.

Lamps

Lamps are a nice addition to any space because of the quality of light they give off. The warm illumination on a tabletop and the items it holds brings a welcome feeling to a room—perfect for an entry.

Round Entry Rug

The style of the two rectangular rugs already in place competes with the soft curves of the architecture in the room. Instead of purchasing an area rug, we found just the right carpeting style and had the carpet store cut a circle and bind the edges. It turned out well and was much less expensive than a pre-made circular area rug of an equivalent quality.

Organic-Shaped Mirror

For something fun and unexpected, we had a mirror cut to fit around the light switch and reflect the curved shapes that filled the room. Contact a local glass shop to do the cutting for you, and give them a paper template in the size and shape you want.

Projects

Painting Doors and Trim

One of the easiest and most inexpensive ways to freshen up a room is to paint the walls and trim. Dollar for dollar, a gallon of paint is one of the most versatile decorating tools available.

If you have decided to paint your door trim, somewhere down the road you may be tempted to paint the doors as well, especially if they are plain. If you paint them once, they will have to be painted from that point on, so be sure that you really want to paint them.

Painting doors can be tricky, especially making even paint strokes without a lot of drips or sagging. The secret to any painting project is in the preparation. First, remove any hardware or tape around the entire knob with painter's blue tape. If the door has never been painted, stained or sealed, you will need to prep the surface. Lightly sand with 220-grit sandpaper. Remove dust with a tack cloth or damp rag and prime with a primer sealer. Don't be too concerned with the way you apply the primer. The top coat will smooth out any streaks or uneven areas. If the door has been painted before, sand the surface with 220-grit sandpaper to remove any gloss so that the paint will adhere. Remove dust and spot-prime any bare wood that was exposed while sanding.

When all the prep work is finished you can begin to paint the top coat. Oil-based products level better and don't show as many brush marks, making them a good choice for doors and trim. However, some latex paints now resemble oil-based products as far as leveling and eliminating brush marks. Latex paints can be cleaned up with soap and water, compared to using paint thinner for oil-based paints. Latex paint can be painted over an oil-based paint as long as you use the steps for preparation listed above. ■

Flat-Surfaced Doors

1 **Paint the edge** that faces the room first, wiping off any paint that has crept around to the other side.

2 **Paint around** the door knob if you have not removed it. Just cut in around it, then lay off (smooth out) the paint vertically following the direction of the door.

3 **For the front of the door,** use a roller to apply the paint, then lay off with a paintbrush to give a smooth finish. Try to use a mohair roller cover. They cost a little more but have fewer loose fibers that can get into the final paint coat. Roll the paint on the top half of the door to cover at least past the doorknob. Lay off the paint in upward strokes. If you paint down, the top edge of the door will grab the brush. You'll end up with sags and drips along the top edge of the door.

4 **Roll the bottom half,** overlapping a few inches of the top painted area. Lay off from bottom to center, feathering the brush stroke into the previously painted area. ■

Panel Doors

1 Follow the same steps for flat-surfaced doors, but paint the inset panels first using a brush.

2 After all the insets are finished, paint the horizontal sections and finish off the vertical sections. The secret to painting panels is to make sure the paint is laid off in the direction of the wood of the door. ■

Louvered Doors

1 Louvers on doors can be one of the most difficult painting projects to tackle because of the difficulty of getting even coverage and eliminating drips. It might be best to hire a professional painter who will spray the doors with an airless sprayer. The cost would be a lot less than replacing the doors after you have attempted it yourself. But, for those who are confident about their painting skills, there are two options—paint the louvers by hand or spray the doors yourself.

2 To paint the louvers by hand, work the brush into the louvered slats and lay off the paint in the direction of the louver. Make sure to check the back for any paint that has dripped.

3 To spray the doors yourself, rent or purchase an airless paint sprayer. Make sure that the area in which you work will not be affected by overspray, and practice the technique on a board. Small cup sprayers that can be purchased at a home-center store work well for a small number of doors. If you need to paint more than a few, hire a pro! ■

Projects

36" Round Table

SHOPPING LIST
4 x 8 sheet of ¾-inch
  medium density
  fiberboard (MDF)
2-inch drywall screws

MATERIALS ON HAND
Circular saw
Jigsaw
Scroll blade to fit jigsaw
Router with roundover bit
150-grit sandpaper
Dowel compass
Straight edge

Project note

Make sure to wear a particle mask when sanding and cutting fiber board.

1 Starting with a sheet of 4 x 8 MDF, cut the sheet into two sections. One section should be three feet long and the second section five feet long. The board is cut to size using a circular saw. Use a straight edge as a guide for the circular saw to get a nice straight cut.

2 Using a dowel compass, which can be purchased at a home center store, draw a 36-inch-diameter circle on the larger piece of MDF. A long piece of string and a pencil can work well for a compass if you don't want to purchase a dowel compass. This will become the tabletop.

3 Cut out the circle using a jigsaw with a scroll blade attached. Cut slightly outside the line. After you have cut out the circle, sand the edge smooth using the pencil line as a guide. A belt sander can cut the sanding time in half.

4 Using a router with a roundover bit, soften the top edge of the tabletop. Make sure the roundover bit has a bearing wheel to follow the outline of the table.

5 To make the support legs for the table, cut two 29¼ x 30-inch rectangles from the remaining piece of MDF.

6 Make a pencil mark four inches from the top and bottom of both sides, then line up the circular tabletop onto the pencil marks and draw a curve matching the curve of the top. Do this to both pieces.

7 Cut out the curves using the jigsaw with the scroll blade attached. Sand the edges smooth with 150-grit sandpaper.

8 Clamp the two panels together. Find the center of the non curved edge. Draw a ¾-inch slot halfway down the panel, parallel to the curved edges. Cut out the slot with the jigsaw and lightly sand the edges.

9 Assemble the base by sliding the two pieces together. Attach the tabletop to the base by drilling countersunk pilot holes through the top down into the leg unit and then secure using 2-inch drywall screws. For a sturdier top, apply wood glue before attaching if the unit will not be disassembled. ∎

Cantilevered Shelves

SHOPPING LIST
1 x 6 poplar board
1 x 3 poplar board
1 x 2 board
Self-anchoring molly bolts
2½-inch dry-wall screws
1-inch dry-wall screws

MATERIALS ON HAND
Miter saw
Cordless drill
Hammer
Finishing nails
Awl
Nail set
Sandpaper
Spackling compound
Drywall screws
Wood glue

Project note

The shelves in the entryway vary in length. Your project can be any size you choose. The shelf shown here measures 24 x 6 x 3.

1 **The shelves are basically** a rectangular frame. Cut the 1 x 6 to 24 inches in length using the miter saw. **Note:** *the shelf should not be wider than six inches. This is the correct width for the shelf to* be able to support itself and a few accessories in this cantilevered fashion. You will need two lengths of lumber for each shelf.

2 **Cut two side pieces** from the 1 x 3, the width of the 1 x 6. **Note:** *Due to the milling process, most lumber is not the size that is marked on it. Always measure; don't assume that the size marked on the board is the actual size.*

3 **Attach the two side pieces** to one of the shelf boards making sure that they are flush with the top of the board. Use glue and finishing nails to attach them. Then attach the remaining shelf, again making sure that the pieces are flush. You should have two sides, a top and a bottom forming a rectangular box.

4 **Measure the length** of the shelf and cut a face board out of 1 x 3 the length of the shelf. Attach to the front of the shelf unit using glue and nails. Set all nails with the nail set and fill all holes with spackling compound. Sand the shelf lightly with 220-grit sandpaper and paint the color of your choice.

5 **Cut a 1 x 2 piece** of lumber the length of the inside of the rectangular box to form the hanging cleat. This piece should be able to easily slide into the box.

6 **Drill pilot holes** into the cleat. Position the cleat so that it is level on the wall and mark the location of the holes by pushing an awl through the holes. Drill self-anchoring molly bolts into the marked locations and attach the shelf using 2½-inch-long drywall screws.

7 **Slide the shelf onto the cleat** and secure the shelf onto the cleat using 1-inch drywall screws through the top of the shelf. ■

Projects

Round Tablecloth

SHOPPING LIST
Fabric of choice
Thread to match

MATERIALS ON HAND
Sewing machine
Fabric measuring tape
Scissors
Pencil
Iron
Pins

Project Note

To prevent the seam from running down the middle of this tablecloth, the center is made from a full width of fabric with two narrower panels sewn to each side.

1 **Determine the finished diameter** of the tablecloth by adding the diameter of the table and twice the height of the table. Make sure to add extra length if you want the cloth to pool on the floor.

2 **Add 2 inches** to this number for hems. The final number is the cutting length for the center panel. Cut center panel to length determined in step 1.

3 **To determine the cutting width** of the two side panels, subtract both seam allowances (⅝ inch each) from the center panel width. Subtract the finished center panel width from the finished diameter determined in step 1. Divide the remainder by two. This is the finished width of the two side panels. For the cut width, add one seam allowance (⅝ inch) and one hem (1 inch).

4 **Cut the two side panels** to the same length as the center panel, and to the width determined in step 3.

5 **Pin the side panels** to the center panel and sew together with ⅝ inch seam allowances. Press seams open.

6 **Fold the fabric** in half to form a rectangle, then in half again to form a square. Mark the corner that is the center of the tablecloth with a pin.

7 **Draw one quarter** of the circle by measuring out from the corner marked by the pin and drawing tick marks to form a nearly solid line to follow. Cut away excess fabric.

8 **Press under a half** inch hem, twice, and pin into place. Since the tablecloth is round, the hem will need to be eased around the curve.

9 **Sew the hem** with a straight stitch or blind hem stitch. Press. ∎

Framing Family Photos

SHOPPING LIST

Purchased frames to fit several photos

Precut collage matting to fit frames OR sturdy poster board, a metal straightedge and a mat knife

MATERIALS ON HAND

Family photos

Photo mounting tape

Project Note

Many craft or photography supply stores have a huge variety of frame and mat sizes. Look in the scrapbooking section of your local craft store for even more framing ideas.

1 **Place family photos** in an arrangement that makes sense either by person, chronologically or by event. Once the photos are arranged, select a mat configuration that fits, or cut a mat from heavy poster board.

2 **(Optional)** When cutting your own poster board matting, cut the poster board to fit inside the frame first, using a metal straightedge and a sharp mat knife. Lay the photos out on the poster board in your arrangement and lightly mark the corners of the photos with a pencil. Draw the cutting line inside the corner markings so that the opening will be slightly smaller to cover the edges of the photos completely. Cut along the lines and gently erase the pencil marks.

3 **Center the photos** in the openings on the back of the mat or poster board. Use photo mounting tape to secure the photos in place. A piece along the top is usually all that is required.

4 **Remove frame backing** and spacers, and clean the inside of the frame glass. When dry, insert the mat with photos and replace the spacers and frame backing.

5 **Hang your personalized family photos and enjoy.** ■

The Entryway is now a beautiful, functioning space with plenty of storage for day-to-day needs. The family photos bring a sense of history and family into the room, and this entryway definitely sets the direction for an interesting and artistic home.

Before

After

Great Rooms

A relatively new concept in home design, great rooms are popping up everywhere. They are part of an increased interest in open, grandiose spaces. The sprawling two-story walls and windows, though impressive, are a bit more challenging to decorate than a single-story living room.

What's Right?

Before

The Fireplace

The combination of rough, layered stone and smooth, simple moldings gives this fireplace a very warm and welcoming charm. The mantel is painted to match the trim throughout the house, and it contrasts nicely with the earthy tones of the stone. However, against the white walls, the details of the mantel get lost.

The Great Room has become the single offspring of the combination of the living room and the family room. **This one has a lot going for it with the design of the quarter-round windows, the textural stone fireplace and quality furnishings.** Fortunately, the entertainment center already in place is in just the right scale for this room—big!

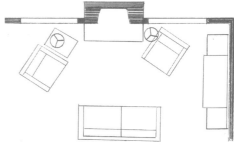

Furniture Arrangement

Using the furniture pieces available, this is the best arrangement considering function and aesthetics. The sofa faces the view and the fireplace, and the "favorite" chair is angled toward the television!

The Entertainment Center

This three-piece cabinet houses the television and all of its components in an organized, efficient and beautiful way. **It is quite large and is in perfect scale with the room,** and the wood tones are rich and lovely, pulling out the deepest colors of the stone.

The Windows

The intriguing shape of the windows and their placement make quite an impact in this great room. They are part of a focal wall that includes the view and the fireplace; the three together make such a strong statement, the rest of the room needs to be striking as well in order to keep this wall from becoming overpowering.

The Upholstered Furniture

All of the upholstery in the room is leather. The sofa and a chair are a matching natural brown, and an additional chair of sentimental value is a rich red. All of the pieces **are in great shape and comfortably broken in.** They are perfect for a room that is constantly occupied.

What's Wrong?

White Walls

White walls show off the expanse of this room, but a color would help emphasize the white mantel and the beautiful textured stone.

Bare Windows

As interesting as the windows are, there are times when the pure sunlight that streams in is too harsh. A window covering that softens the glare will help.

Mismatched Accessories

Once a standard of quality is set, it's difficult to skimp in other areas. Accessories that are appropriate for a basement rec room will look out of place when teamed with a group of high-end furnishings.

Inappropriate Furnishings

The wicker truck currently being used as a coffee table looks out of place. It does not match the quality of the the leather upholstery or the other furnishings in the room.

Let's Get Started!

Find an Inspiration Piece

The best place to start in a room that is going in several directions is with an inspiration piece. **The inspiration piece narrows everything down, giving the room a theme or a story. Each item added to the room must complement and support that story.** A country-styled quilt in just the right colors is the inspiration for this room. Textured and patterned pillows were selected to coordinate, along with rustic plates, wooden bowls and greenery.

Fixes

White Walls?
Paint Them!

Don't be afraid to paint two-story walls. This is a must—these walls really need some color to give this large room some pizzazz. Paint the focal wall in a contrasting accent color for even more impact!

Bare Windows?
Add Blinds!

These woven-wood blinds aren't completely opaque. In fact, some light does peek through. However, the blinds block out enough of the light to allow better TV viewing, less direct sunlight on the furnishings and even some privacy in the evening hours. An added benefit is the texture they bring to a room full of smooth surfaces.

Inappropriate Furnishings?
Time to Trade Up!

Replace the wicker chest with a coffee table from the same furniture collection as the entertainment center to maintain a consistent quality and look. Place a sofa table of similar style against the stair wall to hold additional lighting.

Mismatched Accessories?
Follow Your Inspiration!

A colorful welcoming quilt inspires a comfortable and welcoming room. These rustic, textural accessories add warmth to the space, and the pineapple motif, a symbol of welcome, works beautifully in theme as well as color.

Two-Story Walls

The Focal Wall

This two-story wall is a large presence in both the great room and the rest of the house. A rich caramel accent color pulled from the inspiration quilt helps set apart the window trim and the fireplace mantel. Blinds in the windows and a colorful collage of plates above the fireplace combine to create a striking image worth a second look.

Entertainment Wall

Even though the entertainment center is large, it is not tall enough to fill a two-story wall. This space over the cabinet is the perfect spot for the inspiration quilt. Centered above the cabinet, it covers the excess white space nicely. The addition of the wicker chest and a few silk topiaries on top of the cabinet add interest and break up the linear shapes of the quilt and entertainment center.

Stair Wall

The stair wall already has the built-in character of twisted wrought-iron rails. Hanging artwork that follows the line of stairs brings additional interest to this area. A sofa table placed against the wall provides functional and asthetically pleasing light for the quilt print hanging behind it.

Kitchen Wall

The great room is divided from the kitchen by a partial wall that extends down from the ceiling. Even though the wall is above eye-level, it shouldn't be left empty. A twelve-foot oak shelf decorated with silk greenery, framed artwork and country accessories makes this high wall as pleasing to view as the others in this room.

The Homestretch

When a room that is being decorated is open to other rooms, those rooms should be addressed as well. In this case, the great room was completely open to the kitchen and partly open to the dining room. To complete the great room, the other rooms had to be considered.

Installing coordinating woven-wood blinds in the kitchen creates a more comfortable eating area, since they cut down on glare in this space as well. Accent lighting added to each end of the breakfast bar creates a welcome place to dine. Placing coordinating vignettes of accessories above the kitchen cabinets immediately ties the two rooms together.

The dining room also benefits from the addition of matching blinds, which provide privacy from the neighboring houses during the evening hours. Chandelier shades added to the wrought-iron fixture help soften the lighting. Notice the accessories on the wall shelf—the pineapple is easy to spot, and coordinating dinnerware brings colors and textures from the great room into this space as well.

Projects

Painting Two-Story Walls

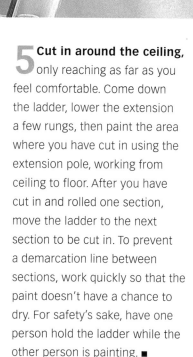

SHOPPING LIST
Latex satin paint

MATERIALS ON HAND
Ladder mitts
Painter's pothook
20-foot extension ladder
Extension pole
Drop cloths
Painting supplies

Project note

Painting two-story rooms isn't much different than painting a normal room—it's just harder to reach. If you're intimidated by heights, you may want to hire a pro.

1 Cover the floor using a 4 x 15 drop cloth. Leave plenty of room on the floor so the ladder can rest on the floor and not on the drop cloth. On wood floors, it may be necessary to place the ladder feet on a nonskid pad. Never place the ladder feet on a drop cloth when working on hardwood floors—the ladder could slide and fall.

2 Place ladder mitts on the ends of the ladder that will rest against the wall to prevent the ladder from marring the wall. Extend the ladder so that it reaches within a couple of feet of the ceiling. Do not make the angle of the ladder too steep. You should be able to stand almost straight up on the ladder.

3 Place a small amount of paint in a plastic pail, just enough to cut in, to prevent spilling a full can from two stories up. Use a painter's pothook to hold the pail in position while you are on the ladder. Using a pothook allows you to have one hand free to paint while you hold onto the ladder with the other.

4 As you climb the ladder, have another adult hold the ladder to prevent slipping.

5 Cut in around the ceiling, only reaching as far as you feel comfortable. Come down the ladder, lower the extension a few rungs, then paint the area where you have cut in using the extension pole, working from ceiling to floor. After you have cut in and rolled one section, move the ladder to the next section to be cut in. To prevent a demarcation line between sections, work quickly so that the paint doesn't have a chance to dry. For safety's sake, have one person hold the ladder while the other person is painting. ■

Quilt Hangers

SHOPPING LIST
1½ x ¼-inch bolt with
    wing nut
1 x 3 oak lumber
Sawtooth picture hangers
Stain or paint in desired
    color

MATERIALS ON HAND
Miter saw
Drill with bits
Spade bit
Clamp
Long level
Sandpaper
Nails and screws

Project note

The size of the quilt to be hung will determine how many hangers will need to be built. Ideally, you should place a hanger at each end of the quilt, with hangers being spaced no more than 24 inches apart in the center.

1 Cut the 1 x 3 into 4-inch-long blocks using the miter saw. Cut two blocks for each hanger.

2 Lightly sand all edges of the blocks with 220-grit sandpaper.

3 Find the center of each block and drill a pilot hole large enough for the bolt to pass through easily. One of the blocks needs to have a counterbore hole large enough for the bolt head to rest in, so that the blocks rest flat against the wall. Drill the hole using a spade bit, drilling deep enough so that the bolt head is completely hidden. **Tip:** *Clamp the block to a workbench to keep it from spinning while you drill.*

4 Stain or paint all the blocks and allow to dry.

5 Attach the sawtooth picture hanger at the top of the back of the block with the bore hole.

6 Lightly mark the location of the quilt on the wall. Use a long level to be sure it hangs straight. Mark the locations where the hangers will be attached to the quilt. Drive nails or screws into these locations.

7 Push the bolt through a block and slip the second block onto the bolt. Position the quilt between the blocks and tighten using a wing nut. Place the hangers over the nails or screws located on the level line. ■

Arranging and Hanging Plates

SHOPPING LIST
Plates to hang
Plate hangers to match
    plate size
Picture hooks

MATERIALS ON HAND
Hammer
Measuring tape
Masking tape

1 To get just the right arrangement of plates for any wall space, measure the space available and mark it with masking tape on the floor.

2 Move the plates in the space on the floor until you have a pleasing arrangement. Generally a vertical or horizontal oval shape works well, as do other geometric shapes for the entire arrangement.

3 Attach the correct size spring-loaded plate hanger to the back of each plate.

4 Start at either the top or the bottom, or with an item that is definitely in the center of the arrangement, and begin hanging the plates on picture hooks. ■

Before

This Great Room now makes a complete decorating statement. The walls, entertainment center and fireplace mantel are all accessorized in a well-thought-out manner. Dressed windows indicate a complete design. Knowing when to stop is easy— it's when everything has been addressed and the room creates a cohesive statement.

After

Dining Rooms

A beautifully designed dining room creates an atmosphere that encourages your guests to linger and chat. You may find your dining room being used more often once it becomes a room you enjoy!

What's Right?

Before

Wainscoting

Detailed wainscoting such as this is time-consuming and can be expensive. When it comes with the house, it's a huge plus! This wainscoting, although not shown in the room photo, is painted in an off-white that matches the rest of the home's trim so it immediately coordinates with the decor throughout. Wainscoting on the bottom of a wall means you only have to decide what to do with the top half of the wall space.

This Dining Room, at first glance, seems to be complete. The furniture is lovely, the wainscoting on the walls and the columns are a nice architectural detail, and the space seems to be well-accessorized. However, the "wow" factor is missing—so let's fix it, one step at a time.

Crown Molding

As a do-it-yourself project, crown molding (not shown in room photo) is **high on the "want" list**, but it also ranks high in degree of difficulty. If your home already has lovely architectural details like this room does, you should be thrilled!

Chandelier

This traditional brass chandelier is nice in combination with the traditional furniture. The polished brass arms and candlestick light fixtures add to the elegance of the room.

Furniture

All of the furniture in this room—the china cabinet, table and chairs—is in excellent condition. The pieces match and they pull the room together nicely. **A new piece in a different style, though, could be a welcome addition.**

What's Wrong?

Before

White Walls

White walls can be an elegant background for a variety of furnishings. However, the bold red walls of the adjacent living room make these white walls seem bland.

Bare Windows

Even if the view outside is pretty and full of foliage that provides privacy, an elegant dining room requires some softness at the windows—not to hide the view, but to frame it, as a curtain on a stage.

Empty Spaces

When there are completely bare wall spaces in any room, they stand out like a sore thumb. This room needs one more piece of furniture placed diagonally across from the china cabinet to balance the room.

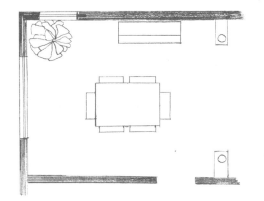

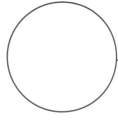

Glaring Chandelier

The style of this chandelier is fine, but the glare from the bare lightbulbs can cause fatigue—the last thing needed at a dinner party!

Let's Get Started!

This dining room is connected to the kitchen with a doorway and is completely open to the living room, so it's important that it coordinates with both rooms. The best way to get started in this dining room is to investigate the color and patterns in the adjoining rooms. By taking a closer look at the finished rooms that surround the dining room, clues can be found that make decorating that room easier. What is most striking about the adjacent kitchen is the black background border at the ceiling. It defines the perimeter of the kitchen and offers a lovely collection of colors to be used for backgrounds and accents in the dining room.

The focus of the red-walled living room is a sofa with a warm floral print. The gold tone background of the fabric mimics the backgrounds from the kitchen and could be a unifying factor for the dining room. Additionally, the green, gold and red from the living room combined with the dramatic black from the kitchen create a new and interesting color scheme for the dining room.

Our choices—
a large-scale floral fabric, medium-scale toile and small-scale check that blend well together and stand out nicely against the striped painting technique.

Fixes

White Walls?
Add Color and Pattern!

Most of the large patterns in and around this room are either fruit or floral designs, so for contrast, a geometric design is best for the walls. A traditional stripe supports the style of the furnishings and the soft cream and gold colors are pulled out of the warm fabric on the sofa in the adjacent living room.

Empty Spaces?
Add Furniture!

A cabinet taller than the height of the table is needed to balance the weight of the china cabinet. We decided on a do-it-yourself wine rack because it could be built to our specifications to both fill the space and a special need. Remember, there's nothing wrong with creating a handcrafted project to help stay within a budget!

Bare Windows?
Frame With Soft Fabric!

Our goal for the window treatments is to preserve the outdoor view while softening the hard edges of the window trim. Inset toppers on tension rods will not harm the wood trim or take away from the view. Stationary side panels add height, warmth and flair.

Chandelier Glare?
Add Shades!

The addition of decorative chandelier shades diffuses the light from bare lightbulbs, which greatly reduces harsh glare. Installing a dimmer switch is a great do-it-yourself project, and lets you control the level of light even further.

Tip: A chandelier is properly installed if the bottom of the fixture hangs five feet above the floor. Check yours with a tape measure.

Add Personality

The Accessories

"The stuff," as Matt calls it, shouldn't be overlooked, or the room won't be complete. The "stuff" is what keeps a living space from looking like a hotel room decorated by formula. When personal accessories are added, the history of the family is brought into the room, making a statement about the people who live there. Think of accessories as the jewelry for a room, or the final touches that turn a well-designed room into a room custom designed for you!

Lighting

Lighting is so important to the function of a room that it is not usually considered an accessory. Lamps with great style like these certainly add to the personality of a room, placing them in the accessory category as well.

Greenery

A large plant like this is a green-thumb accomplishment! Placed in the corner between two windows, the foliage outside is complemented by the greenery inside.

Artwork

Artwork should be selected because it moves you in some way. It should be something you enjoy gazing at or studying, or even something that evokes questions or conversations. These framed pieces work in this dining room because they complement the homeowner's love of fine wines.

Silk Greenery and Flowers

In contrast to the live green plant in the room, silk greenery can be placed in areas that don't have enough natural light to sustain a real plant, such as on top of the china cabinet. Also, live flowers are great for special occasions, but since they don't usually last more than a few days, silk flowers can be a wonderful substitute and they don't need to be watered or pruned.

The Unexpected

The use of something unexpected in a room isn't necessary for the room to function well or be aesthetically pleasing. Adding the unexpected means you've gone that extra mile and done something that no one would ever consider—it's astonishing to see, making your room that much more interesting and personal.

Chair Back Covers

Most people expect beautiful wood dining room furniture suites to have chairs with upholstered seats and carved, spindled or ladder backs. These dining room chairs are no exception, and the addition of more fabric helps soften all of the hard, wood finishes. Tie-on chair back covers accomplish this task nicely. What makes them so great is that they are easy to make.

Unusual Picture Location

Hang a picture on the wainscoting? Try it! The boxes in the wainscoting on either side of the wine cabinet seemed bare, even after everything is in place. Hanging artwork below eye level works in this case and provides the unexpected!

Before

After

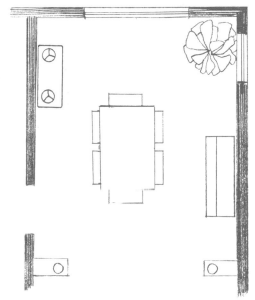

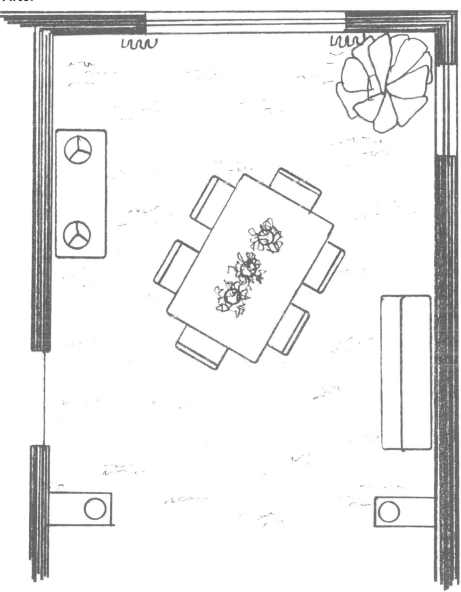

Angled Dining Table

After the backgrounds were in shape, the draperies sewn and installed, the wine rack constructed and the lighting and accessories added, there was still something missing. We stepped back and looked at the room for several minutes, and the thought of an angle came to mind. Two quick tugs at opposite ends of the table and a moment or two to set the chairs back into position, and the dining room was complete! By eliminating the "rows" of furniture running parallel through the space, the regularity has been broken, and the room takes on a completely different look.

Projects

Striped Walls & Painted Ceiling

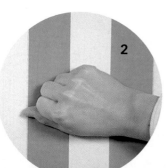

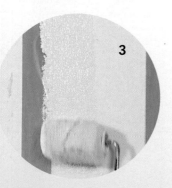

SHOPPING LIST
Main color satin latex paint
(base coat)
Contrasting color latex
paint (for stripes)

MATERIALS ON HAND
Ladder
Drop cloths
4-foot level/tape measure
Painter's blue tape
Pencil
Painting materials

Project note

Before painting, complete the appropriate preparation for the walls and ceiling. Clean the walls, fill holes and remove switch plates and outlet covers.

1 Paint the ceiling first to eliminate drips on the walls. Place drop cloths on the floor, cut in the ceiling and roll on the paint.

2 Mask off any trim before painting the walls with two coats of the base color.

3 Using a long level and tape measure, lay out the stripe lines. Measure 8 inches from a corner and make a pencil mark. Using the level, lightly pencil a line from ceiling to chair rail or floor (photo 1). Work around the room in 8-inch increments until all the stripes have been drawn out. Don't be alarmed if the end stripe isn't exactly 8 inches in width. It won't be noticeable.

4 Start masking off every other stripe with painter's blue tape (photo 2). Press securely so paint won't creep underneath.

5 Using a brush and a roller, cut in the stripe, then roll on the paint, being careful to remain within the taped-off stripe (photo 3). Work your way around the room.

6 Carefully peel away the tape so the base coat is not pulled away with it. Dispose of the tape, remove the drop cloths and enjoy the beautiful room you have just created. ∎

Wine Rack/Buffet Server

SHOPPING LIST

8 (18" x 6-foot) pine panels (can be purchased at most home centers)

L-brackets

Satin-finish latex paint in desired color

Water-based polyurethane (optional)

MATERIALS ON HAND

Router with roundover bit and ¾-inch straight bit

Circular saw

Carpenter's square

Bar clamps

Miter saw

Hammer

Wood glue

220-grit sandpaper

1 x 4 scrap of lumber to build a jig

Paintbrushes

Project note

As with any project, you need an inspiration. We purchased a set of wrought-iron wine racks that we thought would work well in the cabinet. We built the cabinet to accommodate the dimensions of the racks. Your measurements may vary.

1 **The wine rack** has a total of five shelves that measure 18 x 54 inches. Cut the panels to length using a circular saw. Use a long guide to make the cuts. Clamp the guide in position and run the circular saw along the guide. After cutting, soften the edge of the shelves with a router and roundover bit with a bearing guide. Sand smooth with 220-grit sandpaper.

2 **Cut all the dividers/ supports** from the remaining panels. The supports measure 12 x 18 inches. Again use the circular saw to cut the supports to length and width. There will be a total of nine supports for the lower four shelves. The top shelf has three supports that measure 5 x 18 inches wide to create a small book storage shelf.

3 **Now you have the option** of toenailing the supports into position or routing a dado for them to fit into. When toenailing, simply drive the nails into the supports at an angle, so the nail is driven through the support and into the shelf. Toenailing does not give a very strong bond between the two pieces. A dado will allow the support to slide into the groove and be secured with glue, giving a nice tight joint and bond.

4 **To rout the dado,** build a jig out of 1 x 4 scrap pieces of lumber. The jig is just wide enough for the router base.

5 **Assemble the rack** on a flat surface. The back of the shelves and supports should rest on the flat surface. Apply glue in the dadoes of the bottom shelf and slide the supports into place. Continue adding supports and shelves until the top shelf is placed. Clamp and let dry.

6 **The base of the rack** is a 1 x 4 frame that measures 17 inches wide x 34 inches in length. Cut the boards on a miter saw and assemble the frame with glue and nails. Attach to the bottom shelf with 2-inch L-brackets.

7 **Paint the wine rack** the color of your choice, using a satin-finish latex paint. For added protection, coat with water-based polyurethane. ∎

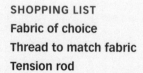

Projects

Flat Scalloped Valance

1 **Determine the finished** width and length of your valance. Ours is 1 inch narrower than the opening of the window and looks right at 16 inches long.

2 **Cut a front and back** panel in the rectangular shape needed, adding a ⅝-inch seam allowance to each side.

3 **Divide the cut width** of the valance into scallops of equal size. Our curves are each 5 inches across. Then, find an object around the house, such as a dessert plate, vase or a school compass that will help you draw even scallops all the way across the bottom edge of the fabric.

4 **Cut the scallops out** of both rectangles. With right sides facing, pin the rectangles together and stitch across the top edge first, leaving an area in the middle unstitched so the valance can be turned right side out after sewing.

5 **At the beginning** of the side hem, leave an opening unstitched, large enough for the tension rod to pass through.

We left a 1-inch opening for ours. Then, stitch the side seams and the scallops, leaving the same 1-inch opening at the top of the other side seam as well.

6 **Trim the seams,** clip slits around the scallops, and then turn the valance right side out and hand-stitch the opening across the top closed.

7 **Iron the valance flat,** insert the tension rod and hang the valance. ∎

Chair Back Covers

SHOPPING LIST
Fabric of choice,
    approximately 4 yards
    per chair
Thread to match
Satin ribbon to match

MATERIALS ON HAND
Marker or pen
Scissors
Sewing Machine

1 Begin by laying the back of the dining chair flat against a piece of paper large enough to make a pattern, and trace around the back of the chair. Cut out the pattern.

2 Pin the pattern to the fabric and cut four of the pattern pieces, two for the front panel and two for the back panel, adding a 5/8-inch seam allowance around all edges.

3 Determine where to locate the satin ribbons to best hold the covers in place. We selected seven different positions, three across the top and two on each side.

4 Cut two 9-inch pieces of satin ribbon for every location. Pin one piece ribbon in each predetermined place along two of the fabric pieces. Pin them to the right side of the fabric with the ribbons extending to the center of the fabric, not to the outside.

5 With right sides facing and ribbons to the inside, pin two pattern pieces together—one with ribbons, one without. Sew the panels together leaving an opening at the bottom to turn the panels right side out.

6 Trim the seams, clip the curves and turn the panels right side out. Iron flat and hand-stitch the opening closed.

7 Tie two panels onto the back of each dining chair and start bragging. ■

Arranging Vignettes in a China Cabinet

Think about your china cabinet as if it were a glass merchandise cabinet in a store. All of the items displayed within need to be shown in their best light, as if for sale. It is important to create interesting vignettes that will still allow you to store most of your dinnerware and serving pieces. It's possible to show off a 12-piece dinnerware service, if your china cabinet is like this one. Just treat each window as a picture frame, and create a piece of art within. Use plate stands to show off pretty dinnerware patterns. Try cup and saucer stands that allow the interior of the teacup to be seen. Add unique items for interest as well, such as silk flowers, framed art pieces, salt and pepper shakers, etc., that break up the sea of porcelain and glass. If your china cabinet doesn't have glass shelving and lighting recessed in the top, see if it's possible to make the change. It can become a lovely accent light in the room during a meal, while being the prettiest piece of art in the room! ■

After

Before

This Dining Room may not be your style, but you can't deny that positive changes have been made. It is especially difficult to make improvements when a room starts out in good shape. Just treat it like any other decorating project where the goal is to turn a dream into reality!

Kitchens

"The kitchen is the heart of the home." That may be a well-worn cliché—but it's hard to deny! Because it is the most utilized room in your home, decorate your kitchen with the same consideration as you would any other room.

What's Right?

Oven Fan

While the copper oven fan was a sore spot in the contemporary colors of this kitchen, the richer hues and country motifs chosen for the new decor will make it a real gem!

Before

This Kitchen is decorated in colors that were an attempt at a contemporary color palatte even though the cabinets are rustic in style. **Now several years later, the contemporary palette looks dated. This is a perfect example of the disadvantage of simply following the trends.** Since the kitchen will be redecorated with a more classic country look, the new design of the room will stand the test of time.

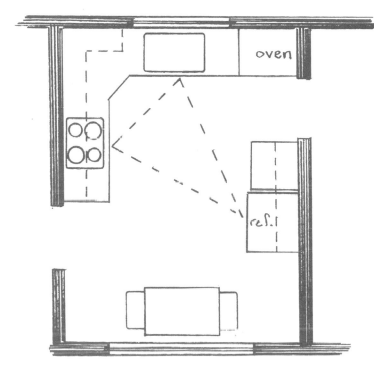

oven

ref.

Floor Plan

As far as function, storage space and size, this room is great! **The ideal kitchen workspace triangle** (which is the distance between the sink, stove and refrigerator) **should measure between 12 and 27 feet** (the total of each of the three measurements of the triangle). In this kitchen, the workspace triangle measures less than 20 feet.

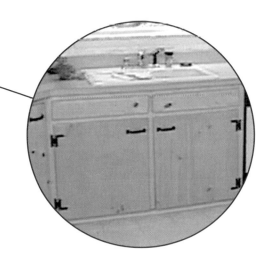

Cabinets

The cabinet underneath the cooktop holds pot lids neatly, and also contains slots for cookie sheets—a great feature in any kitchen. But while the insides of the cabinets are storage wonders, the outsides do need work.

What's Wrong?

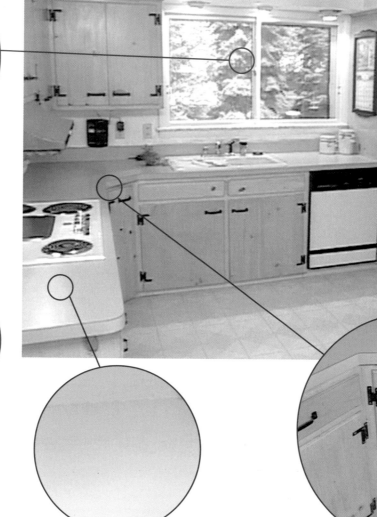

Before

Bare Window

In a kitchen where hard surfaces prevail, add softness to windows in the form of pleated fabric shades, window toppers, Roman shades or even wooden shutters.

Plain Background

Solid color walls that nearly match the cabinets don't add any personality to this space. The same could be said for the white vinyl floor. The lack of contrast and pattern makes everything blend together. The result—a room with no interest.

Trendy Countertop

Colored countertops are a great idea—just be careful which color you choose. Teal is a trend color. A traditional color, such as navy, brown, black or hunter green, is more versatile for such a dominant surface in the room.

Outdated Cabinets

The blond wood of these cabinets was pretty when they were installed. Years later, the flat-panel doors and hardware look outdated and they need a facelift.

Let's Get Started

A kitchen can be one of the most expensive rooms to redo. **A serious "wants" list, divided into do-it-yourself projects and those needing professionals, will help budget planning.** Keep this in mind as well—there are all sorts of options available. Paint can update nearly every surface of your kitchen from cabinets to counters to appliances. To make sure you select the right finishes, find an appropriate inspiration piece.

Do-It-Yourself

Material Cost

Paint cabinets

Change lights

Sew window toppers

Add hardware

Put up wallpaper

Professional

Material + Labor Cost

New countertops

New flooring

Inspiration

A new wallpaper with a folk-art village print is the inspiration for decorating this room. The wallpaper also contains apple motifs that are a fun, subtle connection to the homeowner, who is a teacher.

Flooring Options

When it comes to selecting flooring, personal preference should prevail. Consider first how the floor will function for the space, then consider aesthetics.

Countertop Options

The choice of countertop is usually determined by cost. All price options offer functionality, color range and texture, so choose the best quality you can afford.

Fixes

Wall Coverings

Flooring

Countertop

Window fabric

Cabinets

Plain Backgrounds? Add Pattern and Color!

When we looked through the wallpaper book, we found six coordinated prints and chose the two shown. The subtle blue and beige ticking stripe is the perfect background for artwork and accessories. The busy folk-art village print offers all sorts of colors and design motifs to feature in the rest of the room, and will look great placed below the chair rail. Varying the way you use wallpaper gives your room a custom look.

Painted cabinets allow more options for flooring. Anything from wood to tile to vinyl is appropriate. In this home, the adjoining dining and living rooms have wood flooring. We've chosen ceramic tile for the contrast and texture it adds to the room.

A complementary color scheme consisting of blue and orange keeps this room exciting. Remember, brown, rust and beige are all part of the orange family.

Bare Windows? Add Fabric!

Pocket-gathered valances add softness to the tops of both the windows in the kitchen. Long ties made from simple twine are tied evenly spaced across the top of the fabric valance, creating a soft swagged look. When the pleated blind is raised, it is out of sight behind the topper, giving each window a finished appearance that doesn't hide the view.

Outdated Cabinets? Update the Style!

A painted and distressed cabinet finish coordinates with the primitive country theme of the wallpaper. A new antique-finish kitchen table and chairs completes the look.

Trendy Countertop? Choose Classic Color!

To give this room some pizzazz, a bold deep denim blue laminate was selected. This color coordinates nicely with the wallpapers and is versatile enough to blend with a variety of decorating styles.

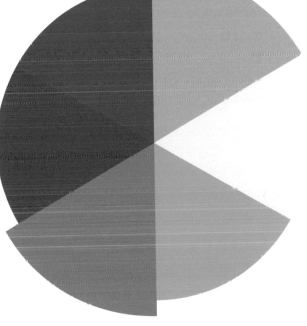

Complementary colors, such as blue and orange, are those opposite each other on the color wheel. Combining these opposing colors for the color scheme of a room produces exciting harmonies.

Fixes

Lighting

These punched-tin light fixtures have interesting shapes, and the punches give them real style. They work perfectly with the primitive theme of the kitchen. Small twig napkin rings placed around the candlesticks add even more character.

Furniture

This antique pie saver looks custom-made for the kitchen. The wood tone is lovely with the antique table and rush-seated chairs. As for the punched-tin panels—one look at the new light fixtures and you know they were meant to be used together!

Add Personality

Accessories

While non-essential in any room, accessories seem even less important in a kitchen, but **the accessories are what give a comfortable kitchen its appeal**. This primitive country-styled room gets added personality from a stack of antique sugar buckets, woven baskets and heirloom ceramic figurines. Keep accessories to a minimum on the countertop. A few plants in the corners add life, and a strategically placed picture or basket hides unattractive outlets.

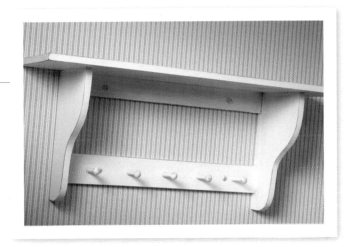

Wall Shelf

A wall shelf offers the ability to create a dimensional design on the wall. More versatile than a framed picture, a wall shelf comes to life with collectibles, candles, baskets and berries.

Table Settings

The most welcoming part of the kitchen is the pretty table decor. Handmade place mats and napkins are beautiful, and a simple electric candle surrounded by a berry wreath adds additional color and interest.

Projects

Distressed Wood Cabinets

SHOPPING LIST
Semigloss latex paint
Semigloss water-based
    polyurethane sealer
Latex primer

MATERIALS ON HAND
Palm sander with 150- and
    220-grit sandpaper
Painting supplies
Wood compound
Tack cloth or damp rag

1 Remove doors and all hardware (photo 1). If you're not replacing the hardware, store it in plastic bags to keep it together. If you are planning to replace the hardware, fill all holes flush with wood compound (photo 2).

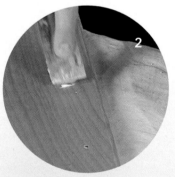

2 Wash all surfaces with a mild soap and warm water solution. Rinse well to remove all soap residue.

3 Sand all surfaces with a 220-grit sand paper. Remove dust with a tack cloth or damp rag. Prime all bare wood with a latex primer.

4 Apply two coats of latex semigloss paint. Paint the doors by using a roller, then lay off the paint with a nylon bristle brush (photo 3), working from the bottom up. Use a brush to paint the cabinet casing. *Note: "Laying off" is a term that means to pull the brush through the paint in long even strokes. It is best to lay off in the direction of the grain of the wood. The inside walls of the cabinet are a great place to practice rolling and laying off.*

5 To distress, use a palm sander with a fine-grit sandpaper to sand off the paint from hard edges of the cabinet doors. Select places that would get heavy use, such as around handles and where the door edges would be grabbed (photo 4).

6 Apply a coat of semigloss water-based polyurethane. Water-based products won't yellow, so they are perfect to use with light colors. ∎

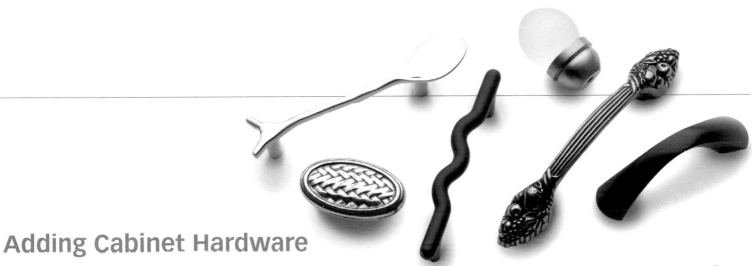

Adding Cabinet Hardware

Project note

When purchasing new hardware you have a variety of options on how and where to install. If you are working with older cabinets where the holes have already been drilled you can purchase hardware that will fit the existing holes, or existing holes can be filled and new locations can be drilled. With new cabinetry, holes will need to be drilled.

The toughest part of installing new hardware is to make sure all the holes are drilled in the same location for every door or drawer. An eighth of an inch off can be quite noticeable and throw off the look of the entire kitchen or bathroom. Trust me. I did just that when I was changing some hardware at my brother's house, and it still bothers me.

The old adage, "measure twice, cut once" fits this project precisely ... except in this case it's measure three times, drill once. When you have established the location of the new hardware, measure the distance between the holes (unless you are using knobs that only have one hole). If this measurement is not precise, the handle will not line up with the holes and the screws will not fit.

1 **Measure in from the edge** of the cabinet and mark the top hole. Measure down from that location the distance between holes. Using the carpenter's

square, line up the two holes so that they are plumb for vertical handles or square for horizontal handles. Double check the layout using the tape measure, measuring in from the cabinet edges. Don't forget to measure the distance between the holes a third time!

2 **Start a small pilot hole** using an awl. Place the point on the pencil mark and give it a gentle tap with the palm of your hand. This pilot hole will keep the drill bit from walking (or slipping) and will give you a perfectly placed hole. Drill the hole using a cordless drill and the appropriate bit for the hardware screws. Use the same measurement for all the hardware and be very sure to measure three times.

3 **If this all seems too complicated,** purchase a cabinet knob template from your local hardware or home-center

store. The template has pre-drilled locations for every knob or handle imaginable. Side and top plastic stops ensure straight and level holes every time. Place the template at the right location, mark the spots with the awl and drill the holes. It's that easy. ∎

Projects

Simple Country Curtain

A lovely, gathered fabric panel tied with one or two grosgrain ribbons or jute twine is a perfect embellishment for a window in a country-themed room. Iron-on adhesive is a marvelous way to make seams and hems, and it allows people without sewing knowlege to create decorative projects for their homes. Here's how to put one together with or without a sewing machine.

1 **Install a curtain rod** in the location you wish to place the panel.

2 **Measure the width** of the rod plus the returns on both sides. For a lightly gathered window shade, without any seams, you may be able to use one 54-inch width of a decorator fabric. Some fabric even comes up to 60 inches wide! If you really want some fullness, you may want to double the measurement of the rod for the width of your panel. This may require cutting two panels of fabric, splitting one in half lengthwise, and either sewing or adhering the cut pieces to either side of the full center panel. To determine the length of the curtain, you need to make a design decision. Will this curtain ever be lowered to give full window privacy? The panel then has to be long enough to cover the glass. If you want the panel to come about a third of the way down the window, you may only need to add about 12 inches to allow for swagging. Of course, when you are figuring dimensions, don't forget to add extra for seams, the hem and the rod pocket.

3 **Sew the side seams** or use iron-on adhesive. Fashion a rod pocket without a ruffle at the top so that the ribbons will lie smoothly over the rod. The best dimension for a 1-inch curtain rod pocket is 1½ inches from seam line to fold. This might be a little trickier when using iron-on adhesive. Add a hem and install the panel on the rod.

4 **Create ribbons** from coordinating or contrasting fabric to gather the curtain into a swag. For a country look, try using grosgrain ribbon, jute or twine. ∎

Homespun Place Mats

1 For each place mat, cut one 12½ x 18½-inch piece of fusible quilt batting, one 12½ x 18½-inch inch piece of fabric for the backing and four 9½ x 6½-inch pieces of coordinating fabrics for the top

2 Using a ¼-inch seam allowance, sew together two 9½ x 6½-inch pieces of fabric along the 9½-inch length; press seams open forming a 9½ x 12½-inch pieced unit. With right sides facing and center seam lines matching, sew together two pieced units to form the 18½ x 12½-inch pieced place mat top.

3 Layer backing, batting and top, then fuse according to manufacturer's directions.

4 Lay the jar lid or plastic circle template at each corner and trace around the edge to create a rounded corner. Trim with scissors.

5 Pin bias plaid binding around outside edge on front of place mat and stitch into place. Turn binding to underside and pin raw edge under; stitch in place. ■

Project note: *Matching napkins can be made by cutting an 18-inch-square piece of coordinating fabric, stitching around each side about ¼-inch from the edge, and unraveling the end threads to create a fringe.*

Before

If this Kitchen could talk, it would just say "ahhh." The new primitive country style blends well with the rest of the house and fits like a glove with the style of the cabinets and appliances. Reserve trendy colors and styles for accessories that can be changed inexpensively as compared to a countertop or flooring.

Bathrooms

Although it is one of the most frequently used rooms in the home, a bathroom is often forgotten when it comes to decorating. How you look as you start each day usually begins right here. The bathroom should energize you, refresh your spirit and help you feel your very best.

What's Right?

Tub Surround

The tub in this bathroom (not shown in room photo) is surrounded by a carpeted step. This step makes the height of the tub seem lower and more approachable, making it easier to get in or out of the tub, and it offers a soft seat. It's a great idea!

Before

This Bathroom has many things right about it. **The long, spacious countertop with double sinks** and the tub that appears sunken are two **bathroom favorites.** The window lets in a lot of natural sunlight to make the space look even larger, and wall-to-wall carpeting (not often used in a bathroom) adds comfort and absorbs sound. All this room really needs is a little decorating!

The Windows

Natural light and fresh air are big bonuses in a bathroom, and this window allows both. It requires careful thought to ensure privacy, and maybe even a layering effect with window treatments to add beauty.

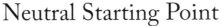

Double Sink/ Full Wall Mirror

Isn't this is everyone's dream for a bathroom? **How wonderful to have the storage and space offered by this arrangement,** not to mention the double sink! There's plenty of room for both his and her toiletries, along with room for the frivolous stuff—the accessories!

Neutral Starting Point

Not enough can be said for decorating a room that starts out with neutral walls, floors and fixtures. **Homes with white walls and oak cabinets may seem to be at a color disadvantage, but imagine the alternatives.** This room could have a blue toilet and a bright pink sink! With neutrals, the options are almost limitless.

What's Wrong?

Before

White Walls

Although they are a good starting point, try not to finish with white. There are all sorts of colors that are nice in a bathroom. Warm, light tones will make you look your best, but anything that coordinates with your inspiration will be better than indecisive white.

Stark Windows

The metal blinds on these windows do control privacy and light, but they are cold and harsh like the rest of the room. This area needs softness.

Storage Issues

Even with all this counter space, favored items end up bunched together in one spot. There must be a better way to use the counter than to completely fill up one corner and leave the middle area empty.

Unsuitable Lighting

The theater lighting that was added to this bathroom when the home was built was attractive then, but the new design requires more stylish fixtures, perhaps with brass arms and glass shades.

Let's Get Started!

Since the function of a bathroom is paramount, it should be considered first. Fortunately, this room was working very well for this family—it just needed a new style direction. **The first step was to find some inspiration.** Since this bathroom is directly off the master bedroom, that became the place to start.

Tie to the Master Bedroom

The master bedroom was just recently decorated in a light country theme. The walls were painted with ragged-on blue stripes, and they were topped off with real fabric stars, as if cut from a quilt. The blue and white tones were a good start for the bathroom, but the family was looking for a more organic feeling in the bath instead of the geometric look of the quilt design.

Accessories Spark Inspiration

The search for inspiration continued until bath accessories were found that coordinated with the blue and white bedroom. The artwork and towels introduce a green leaf motif that adds life and pattern to the otherwise dull white room.

Fixes

White Walls?
Add Color and Pattern!

To keep this room light, a washed-on blue glaze is the answer. The framed leaf artwork is intriguing, and a variety of leaf-motif stamps make it easy to add a similar pattern and color to the walls.

Stark Windows?
Cover in Style!

Metal blinds are a good solution in utilitarian spaces. However, this bathroom deserves better. A translucent pleated shade provides privacy, but allows the diffused light of the morning sun to shine through. The stylish sheer curtain contains pockets that can hold fabric or silk leaves, completing the leaf-themed update.

Storage Issues?
Add Shelving!

This bathroom has a lot of horizontal counter space, but only so much will fit on a flat surface. Without constant upkeep, the items on the counter look like clutter. These vertical storage cubbies are the perfect answer. The bottles can be displayed as accessories, and the counter is kept free for immediate needs such as washcloths and soap.

Unsuitable Lighting?
Remove and Replace!

This is actually tougher than it sounds in this bathroom, because the electrical outlet is located over the center of the mirror. To fix it, a 1 x 10 board (cut the full length of the mirror) is installed to cover the hole, and the new fixture is mounted to the routed board.

Fixes

Tub Area
Add Storage and Decor

As functional and well planned as the tub area is, it still needs storage and decoration. Obviously, this is an area requiring towels within arm's reach as well as bath oil, soap, shampoo and loofah scrubbers. To help out, a wall-mounted shelf offers a place for bath towels, but also doubles as an accessory shelf, bringing interest to this part of the bathroom.

Shower Area
Add Texture and Warmth

A separate shower stall enclosed with sliding glass doors is a unique feature of this bathroom. While it adds function to the room, it needs help asthetically! To warm up the area, a few simple adjustments make all the difference. More of the pretty blue, white and green towels are added, a fuzzy textured bathmat is both functional and comfortable, and a simple blue shower curtain brings softness and warmth to what was formerly a rather cool spot.

Toilet Area
Add Color and Interest

The toilet is in a completely separate room within the bathroom, and any decorating treatments need to carry through into this area. The blue wall color ties this small room into the rest of the bathroom. The louvered cabinet above the toilet adds storage and interest, as do leaf prints framed in oak to match the cabinets in the outer portion of the bathroom.

Projects

Wall Technique

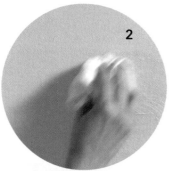

Project note
This wall treatment uses two of our favorite painting techniques, paint washing and stamping.

Washing is one of the easiest painting techniques and stamping is just loads of fun!

1 **Mask off the ceiling and the trim.** Pour one part latex paint and three parts glazing liquid into a paint pail (photo 1). Use a stir stick to mix, and continue stirring throughout the painting process to keep paint and glaze blended.

2 **Dip an old, white gym sock** into the glaze mixture and apply it to the wall in a swirling, "washing" motion (photo 2). (Socks make great painting tools—they're soft and absorbent. If your husband notices some of his favorite ones are missing, just tell him the dryer ate them!) Wash one wall at a time. To highlight some areas, use the same technique to rub on a bit of latex paint right out of the can. Those spots will dry darker and add more interest to the walls. Let the paint cure overnight.

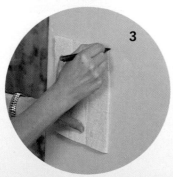

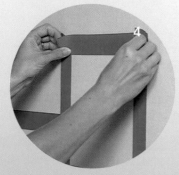

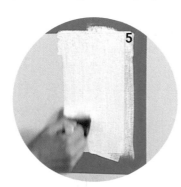

3 Draw an 8-inch square on a piece of cardboard using a carpenter's square; cut out. Randomly place the cardboard square on the walls around the room (using the level to make sure the square is straight) and draw around it with a pencil (photo 3). Mask off the squares with blue painter's tape (photo 4) and fill them in with white acrylic paint (photo 5). Remove the tape and allow to dry.

4 Use a foam brush to apply paint to one of the chunky foam stamps (photo 6). Lightly tap any excess paint onto a paper towel, then press the stamp onto the white squares on the wall using your fingers to press the stamp along the edges. Remove the stamp carefully to prevent smudging the paint. Overlap different stamps using different colors to add dimension and interest to the design (photo 7). ∎

Adding Pockets to Sheers

SHOPPING LIST
**Pair of sheer curtains of
   your choice**
**A third sheer curtain from
   which to cut pockets**
Matching sewing thread

MATERIALS ON HAND
Cutting mat
Rotary cutter
Plastic cutting guide
Pins
Iron and ironing board
Sewing machine

1 Hang the pair of sheers on the intended window, and consider how many pockets are desired and their approximate locations. Mark the center of each pocket location with a pin.

2 Use the third panel of sheers to cut out square or rectangular pockets in the sizes of your choice, cutting them large enough to include a ½-inch seam allowance all the way around.

3 Turn over the top edge of each pocket, folding over ¼ inch twice. This can be helped along by ironing the folds as you go. Stitch the top hem of the pocket in place.

4 Using the iron to help hold the other three side hems in place, fold them each over ¼ inch twice, cutting out some of the bulk at the corners.

5 Place the pockets over the pinned markings on the sheers, and pin the three sides in place.

6 Sew the pockets to the sheers, cutting all loose threads after sewing is completed.

7 Use a variety of items to fill the pockets or leave some of them empty for a more interesting appearance. Silk flowers can be used, shells or leaves are nice, and lettering can provide a lot of entertainment as messages left for loved ones. ∎

Projects

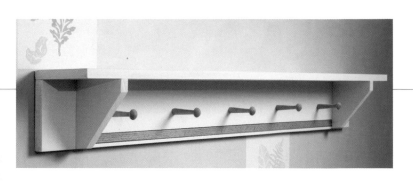

Easy Wall Shelf

SHOPPING LIST
1 x 6 pine lumber
Decorative trim
Wooden pegs

MATERIALS ON HAND
Table saw
Miter saw
Plunge router/router guide
¾-inch straight bit
Drill with bits
Carpenter's square
Hammer
Finishing nails
Wood glue
Spade bits
Awl
Toggle bolts

1 **Using 1 x 6 pine lumber,** cut the top of the shelf and the side board to desired length using a miter saw. (The shelf in this bathroom measures 42 inches in length.)

2 **Rip the shelf and side board** to a width of 5½ inches. (A 1 x 6 board is actually ¾ x 5½ inches.)

3 **Cut two 5½-inch square** shelf supports. With pencil, lightly mark the top and back of the shelf supports. Cut a 45-degree angled corner, leaving one inch on both edges (photo 1).

4 **Make pencil marks** on the shelf where the brackets will be placed. Use a carpenter's square to make sure they are square. This provides end points for the routed groove which will hold the decorative trim (photo 2).

5 **Using a router** with a router guide attached, cut a groove the width of the decorative trim (photo 3). To start the cut, gently lower the router onto the board using the pencil marks for the brackets as a starting point. Make several passes lowering the router bit, until the depth of the decorative trim is matched. (Don't try to cut too deep too fast, it could cause the wood to splinter.) Glue the decorative trim into place (photos 4 and 5).

6 **Attach the two shelf pieces** together by running a bead of glue along the top edge of the side shelf and secure with finish nails. Place the brackets into position and secure with glue and nails. The brackets will now conceal the ends of the decorative trim (photo 6).

7 **Drill pilot holes** for the decorative pegs using a spade bit the same dimension as the peg. Space the holes evenly between the two shelf supports. Glue the pegs into position except for the two end pegs.

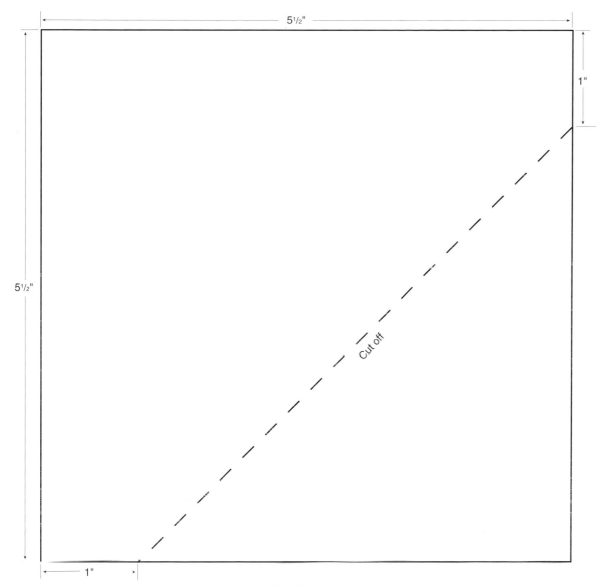

5½"

1"

5½"

1"

Cut off

Easy Wall Shelf Support

8 To install the shelf, use toggle bolts to be sure that it will support the weight of towels. Drill pilot holes through the two end peg holes. Place the shelf into position on the wall, making sure that it is level. Using an awl or long nail, push through the pilot holes to make a location mark on the wall. Set the shelf aside and use a spade bit to drill two holes large enough for the toggle to pass through. While holding the shelf in place, pass the two toggles through the holes until they catch on the other side of the wall. Then tighten the screws while keeping pressure on the toggle pulling the shelf tight to the wall. Readjust for level and glue the last two pegs into place. ■

Children's Rooms

Here's your chance to be a child again. Use your imagination to create a wonderland suited to your child's talents and interests. Get your children involved and have some family fun!

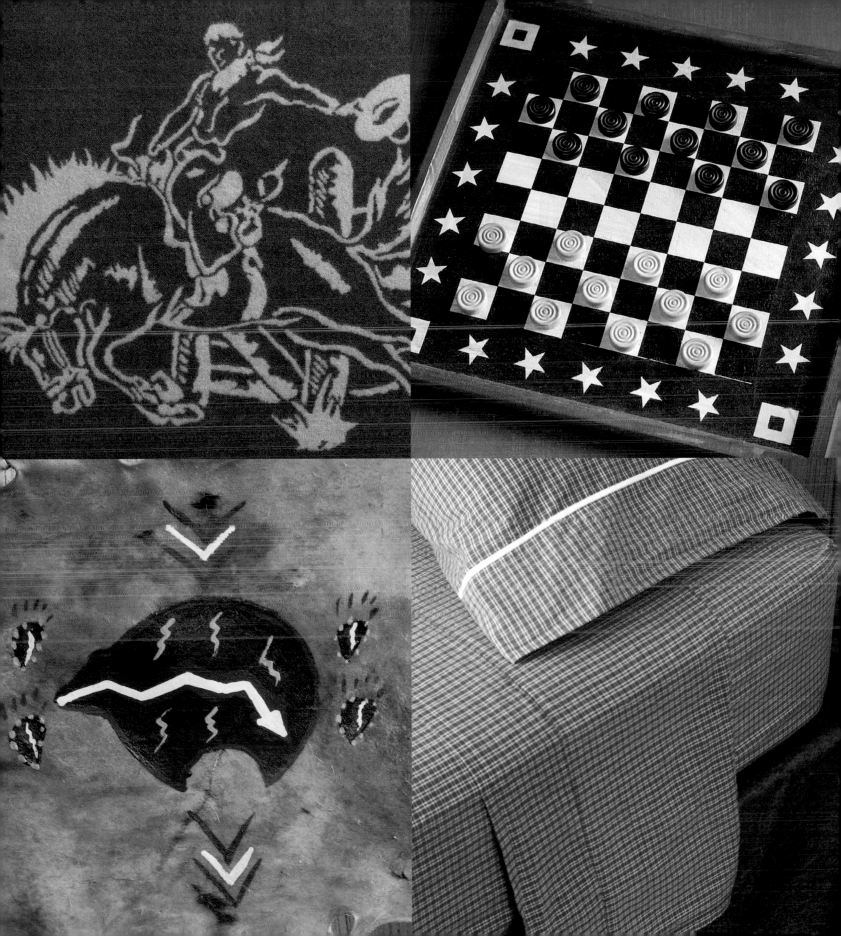

What's Right?

Sound Background

Clean, undamaged walls that are painted or primed are the perfect surface to start with. Clean trim and carpet is a bonus as well.

Furniture

This pair of oak twin beds can be made into a bunk bed. However, separating them allows the children their own private spaces.

Before

This Children's Room has lots of potential. At this point, anything goes. As your imagination runs wild, it's easy to forget about function. Make sure to include room for a desk, play areas, toys and clothing storage.

What's Wrong?

White Walls

Especially in a child's room, white walls are all wrong. Kids love color, shape and stimulation. White walls need to go!

Before

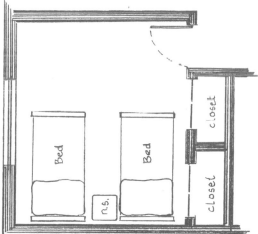

Furniture Arrangement Problems

In the current arrangement, the beds are very close together and one is quite close to the closets. The other end of the room isn't being used at all.

Bland Lighting

Many bedroom ceilings have a single center light fixture. This is effective as general lighting, but can be replaced with a fan and light kit or track lighting.

Window Coverings

Traditional pinch-pleated draperies are great for a more formal space. As the new decor develops, a more appropriate window covering will too.

Let's Get Started!

This children's room was designed for young twin boys. **Each desired a space of his own, with common areas they could share.** Since they are young, areas for play and toy storage are currently more important then a study area.

An activities list can keep a design plan on course, making sure function is addressed. Across from each activity, list what is needed. Then take an inventory of what you have on hand. This method narrows down the shopping list to the essentials!

-Twins' Room-

Activities
- Sleeping
- Playing board games
- Floor play
- Personal space

Needs
- Single/bunk beds
- Table & chairs
- Open space
- Separate toy & clothing storage

Inventory
- 2 single beds
- Nightstand

Shopping
- Table & chairs
- Toy storage

Inspiration

Even though the decorating in a room should be secondary to function, it's hard to resist shopping for ideas for a child's room. As in the three themed groupings below, start with one item that excites your child. It can be a color-block throw, favorite books or even a butterfly border. Build on that one item by mixing in fun colors and patterns, texture and accessories.

Thoroughly Modern Millie

Older children are more aware of trends. All of these decorative items were found at one discount store. Retailers are doing a great job of providing coordinating products for home decor, making it easier than ever to decorate.

Wild, Wild West

Some themes take a little more work. This combination of cowboy and American Indian toys and memorabilia was found at toy stores and antique shops. Collecting these items was fun and educational.

Butterfly Garden

Generally, girls love anything pink. Fortunately, there are hundreds of products available in pink, from ponies to princesses, flowers to fairies. Pink can be frilly, fashionable and fun!

Fixes

White Walls?
Add Paint!

A rough, Western-style texture is right for the Wild, Wild West theme of the room. Painting the walls to resemble rough-sawn cedar planks keeps the color light, yet brings much-needed texture to the background.

Bland Lighting?
Investigate Alternatives!

Track lighting is an easy do-it-yourself project as long as you follow instructions and safety procedures. Turn off the power at the circuit box before starting. If you replace a center ceiling fixture with track lighting, the room will transform from flat to dimensional in no time at all.

Furniture Arrangement Problems?
Draw a Floor Plan!

This furniture arrangement provides a larger private space for each child, which includes their bed and half of a combination nightstand and toy shelf. The closets are easier to access, and there is much more open space for play.

Window Coverings Too Formal?
Go Casual!

To ensure all of the great accessories will take center stage in the room, the backgrounds need to blend together. Wood slat blinds that match the wood trim were installed for light control and privacy. The tabtop curtains blend with the wall color and are lightly textured to help bring a feeling of warmth and some softness to the room.

Theme Building

Cowboy Blanket

When you decide on a theme for the room, look through all sorts of mail order catalogs for items that fit the theme. This adorable wool cowboy blanket was found in a children's furnishings catalog. The earthtone hues work well with the wall color and the cowboy motif sets the tone for half the room.

Cowboy Shelf

Collectible items can be used to decorate a child's room if they are placed well out of reach. This shelf is mounted high above the headboard and acts as a theme builder. A horseshoe photo frame, real spurs and a horse figurine are a few of the collectible items that help set the tone of the room.

Works for Both

Some items fit both the cowboy and the American Indian themes and help tie the room together. The stagecoach lamp, stenciled benches, rich red flannel sheets and wall-mounted hobby horses work well for both sides of the room.

American Indian Blanket

Traditional motifs with a child-like quality cover this wool blanket and add bright colors to the American Indian side of the room.

American Indian Shelf

As if riding to greet him, an American Indian figurine faces the cowboy, adding to the collectible treasures that define this half of the room.

Projects

Rough-Sawn Planking

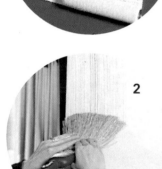

SHOPPING LIST
Dark brown latex satin paint for base coat
Light tan latex satin paint for top coat
Brown paint pens (you'll need several)

MATERIALS ON HAND
Paint roller and tray
Whisk broom
Painting supplies
Drop cloths
Long level and pencil

1 **Mask off the ceiling** and all the trim using painter's blue tape. Lay drop cloths on the floor.

2 **Base coat the room** with latex satin paint. Two coats may be required depending on the color beneath.

3 **Apply the top coat** by cutting in only a couple of feet at a time and rolling a 2-foot-wide vertical section from ceiling to floor (photo 1).

4 **Immediately pull a whisk broom** through the paint from ceiling to floor, wiping off the excess paint from the whisk broom after each pass. To get a nice even stroke, pull the broom with one hand and apply light pressure to the bristles with the other hand. Move quickly so the paint doesn't set up (photo 2).

5 **After completing a section,** move quickly to the next, overlapping the paint on the last section to blend along the wet edge. This technique works best if you can paint one whole wall without stopping. If the edge of one section dries before you start the next one, this will

cause a noticeable overlap and untextured area.

6 **Once the top coat** has dried, lightly mark horizontal lines around the room using a long level and a pencil. Space the lines randomly from 6 to 8 inches apart to create the illusion of rough-sawn planking.

7 **Using brown paint pens,** draw over the pencil lines. This can be done freehand to give a more rustic appearance.

8 **Randomly draw** in vertical lines to represent the ends of the boards. Draw small circles to create nail heads (photo 3). ∎

Track Lighting

Project note

Track lighting is a great way to add task or accent lighting to a room. The fixtures can be moved along the track and pointed in a specific direction to highlight a child's artwork or toys.

1 **Determine the amount** of track you need. Most track comes in 2-, 4- or 8-foot sections. It is best to lay out the design on the ceiling using a long level. Work from the junction box on the ceiling and draw out the desired configuration. We have found that "H" patterns work well. Make sure that you also purchase the

required fittings that attach the track together. Most home center stores have diagrams to help determine the proper fittings and track.

2 **Before you begin,** turn off the power to the room at the circuit breaker or fuse box. *Tip: If you are working alone, plug a radio into an outlet in the room and turn up the volume so you can hear it at the circuit box. When you turn off the correct circuit breaker the radio will stop playing.*

3 **Remove the old light fixture** and check the wires with a circuit tester to make sure they are not live. Start connecting the new track wiring. Most of the time you will simply be connecting white to white and black to black. Make sure you also connect the ground wire.

4 **Tuck any circuit** and fixture wires into the junction box and install the mounting plate to the box.

5 **Snap the track into place** on the junction box. Align the track along the pencil lines drawn on the ceiling, hold in place and mark holes by pushing the awl through the hole into the ceiling. Screw self-anchoring molly bolts into the ceiling at the awl marks. Place the track back into position and secure with screws. Attach any angle, "T" or straight fittings at the end of the track and continue installing track following the layout.

6 **Attach the electrical** adapter to the track by inserting it into the track and twisting. Install the cover over the adapter and mounting plate assembly.

7 **Insert the fixtures** into the track. Turn on the circuit breaker and test the lights.

8 **To add more** interest, install an appropriate track lighting dimmer, so lights can be raised and lowered for extra effect. ■

***Project note:** The light fixtures get hot fast. Don't try to remove a fixture while the light is on. Let it cool. Make sure the fixtures are placed away from draperies and other objects.*

Projects

Night Stand & Toy Shelf

SHOPPING LIST
3 (8-foot) 1 x 12 boards
2 (8-foot) 1 x 3 boards
12 feet of ¼-inch trim
24 x 48 glued-up wood panel
20-inch length of 1 x 8 board
Paint or stain in desired color
Water-base polyurethane
  (optional)

MATERIALS ON HAND
Table saw or circular saw
Band saw or jigsaw
Hammer and finish nails
Carpenter's compass
L-brackets
Wood filler
Sandpaper
Wood glue
Belt sander
Clamps

Project note

Both poplar and pine work well in this project. If you'd like to use a stain finish, use poplar.

1 Cut 1 x 12 poplar or pine boards to three 6-foot lengths for the shelving. Cut three 6-inch lengths for the upper supports and three 9-inch lengths for the lower supports.

2 Clamp all three of the 6-foot shelf boards together (photo 1). Clamping the boards together ensures that all three will be cut exactly the same. Using a carpenter's compass, round off both ends of the clamped boards (photo 2) and cut all three boards at the same time using a jigsaw (photo 3). Do not remove the pencil line when cutting.

3 While the boards are still clamped together, sand the curve using a belt sander (photo 4). Be careful to keep the sander flat so that all three boards are sanded equally. Sand to the pencil line.

4 Working from the bottom up, attach the two side supports to the top of the bottom shelf, 3 inches from the curved front edge. Run a bead of glue along the support edge and nail in place from the bottom. Add the center support in the center of the bottom shelf.

5 Glue and nail the middle shelf to the lower shelf supports. Make sure that the shelves are lined up at each end.

6 Glue and nail the upper shelf supports to the top side of the middle shelf. You will need to toenail, or nail at an angle, the supports to the shelf. The nails will hold the supports in place until the glue has set and dried.

7 Glue and nail the top shelf to the upper shelf supports, again making sure to line up all the shelves. A long level works great for this.

8 To help hold the supports in place, cut small quarter round trim to the shelf width and attach to both sides of the support with glue and nails.

9 Cut 1 x 3 into two 12-inch lengths and two 46-inch lengths. Glue and nail the pieces together to create a frame that will become the bottom base of the shelf unit. Attach the frame to the bottom of the shelf unit with 2-inch L-brackets.

10 **For the table extension,** cut 24 x 48 glued up wood panel into two pieces measuring 24 x 24 and 24 x 20. Round the front edges of the 24 x 24 panel. Cut the curve using a jigsaw with a scroll saw blade attached for a nice smooth cut.

11 **Glue and nail the top** panel to the 24 x 20-inch leg panel, 4 inches in from the rounded edge.

12 **Glue and nail a 1 x 8** support piece underneath the top and the leg, at the center of both.

13 **Tap in all nails** with a nail set and fill all holes with spackling compound if you decide to paint or wood filler if you want to stain the piece. Let dry, then sand the entire piece smooth with 220-grit sandpaper.

14 **Paint or stain as desired.** The piece can be sealed with polyurethane for extra protection. ■

Beanbag Cubes

SHOPPING LIST
Vinyl or other sturdy fabric of choice
Plastic stuffing pellets

MATERIALS ON HAND
Cardboard for template
Sewing machine
Needle and thread

1 **Draw and cut** out an 18-inch square and a 17-inch square of cardboard to use as template pieces.

2 **Use the larger template** to draw six squares on the back of selected fabric.

3 **Center the smaller template** in one of the larger squares and draw around it. The outside lines are the cutting lines, and the inside lines are the stitching lines. Cut out all six squares.

4 **With right sides facing,** stack two fabric squares together and stitch along inside drawn line. Stitch only from one corner of the square to the other—not to the outside corners.

5 **Stitch a second square** to another side of the first square. Repeat until you have four squares stitched together. Stitch the open side of the fourth square to the open side of the first square.

6 **Sew the fifth square** into the square opening formed by the first four squares, using the pencil lines as a seam guide. Sew three sides of the last square into the remaining opening. Leave this last side open for stuffing.

7 **Trim excess fabric** at an angle across each stitched corner, except for the two corners along open side.

8 **Turn the cube right side out** and pour in plastic stuffing pellets until the cube is very firmly stuffed. Fold in the two seam allowances on the open side and hand-sew together. ■

Teen Rooms

A teenager's room contains a whirlwind of activity and an outpouring of emotions and personality. Let the room be one with the teen ... with your continuing guidance, of course!

What's Right?

Architectural Details

As the ceiling follows the roof line in this bedroom over the garage, the space becomes instantly cozy. The large dormers on one side of the room have storage window seats in them, creating a great place for pillowing! It's the architectural details that **make this room fun to live in and to decorate,** and so much more interesting than a square, box-shaped room.

Before

This Teen's Bedroom has a lot of potential. Much of what is already here looks great. However, the button comforter is several years old, chosen when this teen was about 12, so it's time for an update. **All the room needs is a little more personality,** which can be achieved by the addition of fun accessories and personal belongings!

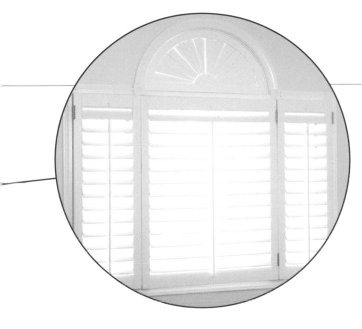

Window Coverings

The design of the window itself adds interest to this room. A good approach to the window treatment **decision takes the design of the windows into consideration.** The white wooden louvers offer light control and privacy and they complement the lovely shape of the window.

Background Colors

This bedroom already has a lovely, restful combination of colors. The deep mahogany-stained wood flooring is found throughout the home and, when combined with the off-white trim, is quite striking. The light aqua selected by this teen as the wall color creates a gentle background perfect for studying and rest.

Walls

Trim

Furniture

At 15, this child received what her parents said was her adult furniture suite, something she could take with her when she moved into her own home. **The style and color were mutual choices,** appealing to both a youthful outlook and an adult concern for function and quality.

Floor

What's Wrong?

Bare Walls

As pretty as this aqua color is, these walls need some artwork that expresses the personality of this teen. Let your children express themselves through their selection of framed or dimensional artwork. If what they choose isn't to your taste, their door can always be kept closed!

Before

Bare Floors

Aside from being hard and cold underfoot, a bare wood floor has no sound-absorbing qualities. When the stereo starts cranking, a thick area rug will muffle much of the sound.

Dated Bedding

Teens will let you know when their rooms are too juvenile for them. The bedding is often what gives the room a childish appearance. Make this change first and the rest of the room will fall into place.

Let's Get Started!

Lighting

Don't ever skimp on the lighting in a room. First consider the tasks at hand, and then address each one separately. This tiny lamp is too short to be placed next to the bed. The style is right, but it appears to be more of an accent light to be used on top of a dresser.

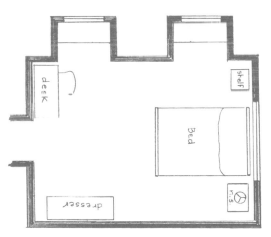

Furniture Arrangement

Placing the bed directly across from the door to the bedroom is generally recommended. However, when that puts the bed in front of a window and creates a "bowling alley" look in the room, try something else. This room will definitely benefit from drawing up a floor plan.

Find an Inspiration Piece

This step should be pretty easy for a teen. **Anything from a favorite music star or sport, to a hobby or decorative item can be inspiration.** Because this teen doesn't want to change the aqua walls, the inspiration piece needs to coordinate. After looking at a variety of different decorative accent pieces, from an oriental rug to a framed flower print to a geometric floral duvet, the duvet was selected. After the duvet was purchased, it was easy to select coordinating accessories.

Fixes

Bare Walls?
Add Interest!

Framed artwork isn't the only addition that can be made to bare walls. Today, anything goes. In this room, dimensional items bring the room alive. Crown molding candle pedestals look great in a group of three. For safety reasons, the candles won't be burned, but their aroma adds a lovely scent to the room. This teen selected an initial plaque for her walls, along with some coordinating posters framed in brushed silver.

Bare Floors?
Add Softness!

White may not be your first choice for the floor in a teenager's bedroom, but this area rug is reversible, so it can last twice as long between cleanings, and that's a plus. With the addition of a pad underneath, the area rug provides softness, sound absorption and warmth to the room.

Dated Bedding?
Find a New Style!
It's a good idea to use the bedding in a room as inspiration. Generally, bedding has a pattern and colors that create a style that can easily be built upon to make decorating a breeze. This is a fun shopping trip to make. Whether you are purchasing fabric to make a bedspread or are searching for a special purchased cover, let your teen select several she would be happy with, and then you help with the final decision.

Inadequate Lighting?
Add or Alter!
Because the style of the original lamp is good, use it as a guide to select a taller lamp with a wider spread of light for the nightstand. The smaller lamp with an oval shade provides enough light for the desk. Even though the shapes are different, the brushed silver metal bases and geometric shades work well together.

Furniture Arrangement Problems?
Rearrange!
This furniture arrangement keeps the bed across from the entry to the room, but places it at an interesting angle. The angle breaks up the bowling alley look, and the room immediately becomes more appealing.

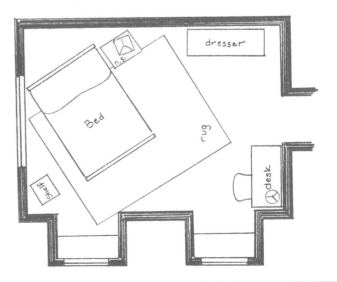

Add Personality

Pillows & More Pillows

Loads of pillows are perfect for nesting. Teen girls accept this concept willingly. Different patterns and shapes also provide visual interest.

Beads

Beads are a fashion accessory today, just as they were in the 1970s. However, instead of hanging them at the window as draperies (what were we thinking), they can now be purchased pre-strung on wire strands to be displayed around windows, furniture legs—and just about anywhere else.

Candles

Candles are more than just for burning. Trim the wicks of candles that will be placed in a child's room so that they can't be burned. They'll still add color, pattern and a wonderful scent to the room.

Organization

Some kids are born organized, but if yours wasn't, you can help instill the need for neatness and order with the purchase of organizational accessories. This organizer unit looks adorable on the desk, and it helps keep stationery, school papers and notes looking tidy.

Flowers

This room with plain-colored walls and clean-lined furniture needs some softness. It is added with the area rug and all of the accessories on these pages. Flowers add an organic touch, bringing color, texture and life to hard lines of a room.

Projects

Painting With a Teen

SHOPPING LIST
Paint
Paint trays
Plastic liners
9-inch roller frame
⅜-inch nap roller cover
Paintbrushes
Drop cloths
Painter's blue tape
Flush spackle

MATERIALS ON HAND
**Boom box and your teen's
    favorite CDs**
Tons of chips and soda pop

1 **Painting with teens** or children of any age can be really fun, but also a challenge. How do you teach teens the proper methods of painting and keep their interest at the same time? The answer is simple: Paint the room with their color selection (you still have the final say of course) and allow them to play their music at the same time.

2 **First coach them** on the proper way to set up the room. Everything that will get in the way must be removed from the room. (See! You'll already be ahead—at least their room will be clean!) Move furniture away from the walls and place in the center of the room. Show them the use of furniture movers (as seen in the How-To Basics chapter). Everything must be covered with a drop cloth (and no, the bedspread is not an acceptable drop cloth).

3 **Show them how** to fill holes flush with spackling (even adults have a hard time with this one, and no, toothpaste does not make a good spackling compound). If you're really brave, teach them how to use a caulking gun. If you don't know how to use one, learn together, but practice in the garage or closet. Show them how to use painter's tape to mask off all the areas that can catch drips, like the baseboard. The prep of the room is where you will lose them. It's boring and tedious, but it's the most critical step. Break up the work into two days. The first day, do all the prep. The second day, paint.

4 **When the prep is finished,** it's time to paint. In a closet or on a wall that is not too conspicuous, teach your teen how to cut in with a brush (cutting in is painting everywhere a roller doesn't fit). The ceiling, the corners of the walls and the trim should all be cut in before rolling. Have them cut in one wall at a time to get the feel of the brush. After the wall has been cut in, let them try their hand at rolling. Show them how not to overfill the roller and how to paint from one corner to another, starting at the top. Roll out the classic "W" pattern and fill in with paint. The biggest mistake all painters make is trying to paint a large surface with one roller full of paint. Fill the roller often.

Rolling will take the most time and patience, but it is the most fun thing to do when painting. Everyone wants to roll.

5 **Once all the painting is done,** show them the proper way to clean up. Remove all the painter's tape right away so the paint film won't adhere to it, making it harder to remove later. Roll up the drop cloths into themselves to prevent wet paint from being brushed on the carpet or furniture. Most importantly, clean all painting tools. (You may want to buy them tools of their own so they will want to make sure that the tools are taken care of properly.)

6 **Most teens want to paint,** for a little while at least. Your job is to make it fun. I always have pizza delivered about midway through the job (I do this even with my adult friends) so there is a fun break time. Play music and be silly. I think the best time I have when working with my crew or friends is the conversation we have while completing the task. What a great way to spend time with your kids, especially when you have paint splattered on your nose. ■

Cutout Lettering

SHOPPING LIST
Paint in desired color
Scrap wood or precut
     wooden letter

MATERIALS ON HAND
Scroll saw
Eye protection
Table clamps
Drill and drill bits
Scissors
Pine lumber
Pencil
Sandpaper

1 **The letters used** in this room were purchased at a home center, but that doesn't mean you can't cut out your own unique letters. All it takes are the right tools, a steady hand and your imagination.

2 **Introducing the scroll saw.** A scroll saw is a table-mounted saw that uses a very fine blade to make intricate cuts on wood or metal. A good model can be purchased for $75–$100. If you are a serious woodworker, you probably already have one of these. If you are just starting out, you may want to attend a class at

a local woodworking store before investing in this saw.

3 **Cutting your own letters.** In a magazine or book or even your computer, find a letter font of your liking. Make a photo copy or print the size of the letter that you want. Cut out the letter and trace it on a piece of pine lumber. (Pine is easy to saw through and can be painted or stained.)

4 **Place the wood** on the scroll saw table and set the blade height. Cut around the letter. To cut inside a letter, drill a pilot hole inside the line and reposition the blade. The beauty of the scroll saw is that the cut is so precise and smooth, very little sanding is required after cutting; just lightly

finish with a 220-grit sandpaper. Paint or stain the letter in the color of your choice.

5 **If you don't want** to purchase a scroll saw, this project can also be done with a jigsaw. The cuts aren't as precise, but the jigsaw does a good job of cutting out the letters. Use a scroll blade in the saw. A scroll blade has many fine teeth and can cut sharper curves than a regular saw blade. You will need to clamp the wood tightly to a work bench and turn the material while cutting. Cut outside the line. Sand smooth, starting with 150-grit sandpaper, and then with a 220-grit paper. Paint or stain with the color of your choice. ■

Projects

Dried Flower Art

SHOPPING LIST
Fresh flowers
Precut mat with four
openings to fit frame
Frame with glass
Two mats cut to fit
precut mat
Thick watercolor paper
to fit frame

MATERIALS ON HAND
Newspapers
Heavy books
Toothpicks
Thick white craft glue

Project note

Flowers are easy to dry. Pick them in mid-morning after the dew has dried and before the heat of the day. Choose flowers that aren't too thick—snapdragons, pansies, nasturtiums, hydrangea and morning glories work well.

Flowers with thick centers, such as black-eyed Susans and daisies can be dried, but will take longer and won't dry as flat as others.

1 Choose flowers to dry.
Place them, one layer thick with space between each blossom, in between sheets of newspaper. Place the sheets of newspaper in between the pages of a heavy book (such as a thick telephone book). Stack more books on top of the book that contains the flowers. Allow flowers to dry for several weeks.

2 After flowers are dry,
carefully remove them from the books and discard the newspaper. On a tabletop, place the flowers in pleasing arrangements that will fit in each opening of the precut mat. When you are happy with the arrangements, transfer them flower by flower, to the watercolor paper. Use a toothpick to apply dots of glue to the backs of the flowers and press them in place; let dry.

3 Remove backing and glass
from frame. Clean glass and let dry. Place two mats in frame. Place precut mat in frame. Place watercolor paper with flowers in frame. Replace backing and hang as desired. ■

Fabric Covered Boxes

SHOPPING LIST
5-inch square papier mache
    box with lid
Cotton or other tightly
    woven fabric
Spray adhesive
Double-stick tape
Acrylic paint to coordinate
    fabric

MATERIALS ON HAND
Ruler
Scissors
Foam paintbrush
Pencil
Iron and ironing board

Project note

This technique can be used for any size box. Simply cut the fabric large enough to cover the width on one side plus one inch and long enough to wrap around two sides and the bottom plus two inches.

1 **Paint inside and outside** of box and box lid with two coats of acrylic paint; let dry.

2 **Cut two pieces of fabric** 6 inches by 17 inches. On one piece of fabric, fold each long edge under ½ inch and press in place with iron.

3 **Spray outside of box** with spray adhesive.

4 **Working quickly** before adhesive dries, cover outside of box with the unfolded strip of fabric by placing 1 inch inside box, wrapping down side of box, across bottom and up second side; tuck the remaining 1 inch of fabric inside box. Smooth excess fabric around corners and press in place.

5 **Place double-stick tape** over the ½ inch of fabric which has been smoothed over painted sides. Repeat step 4 with the folded strip of fabric to cover remaining sides (bottom of box will be covered with a double strip of fabric). Smooth folded fabric edges over double-stick tape and press firmly into place.

6 **Fold raw edge of fabric** inside box under ½ inch twice. Place double-stick tape on back of folded fabric and press in place.

7 **Cover lid** in the same manner. ■

Before

This Teen's Bedroom has certainly changed, and the items added are relatively inexpensive. In fact, the biggest difference was made without spending a dime, by simply changing the furniture arrangement. Updated bedding and some fun accessories take a younger girl's room from OK to awesome!

After

Master Bedrooms

A Master Bedroom is a place to refresh, relax and have private moments. It should reflect a very personal side of you and make you feel better the moment you enter the room.

What's Right?

Furniture

Select good quality, uniquely styled furniture to fill your master bedroom. **Search until you find something that speaks to you personally.** The tricolor stained furniture that takes center stage in this bedroom reflects the homeowner's love of the outdoors. The massive headboard ensures the bed will be the focal point, and the embossed leather panels on the armoire give this bedroom suite a one-of-a-kind look. It's the perfect style and scale for this large 12- by 18-foot bedroom.

Before

This Master Bedroom should say something about its owners, and the piece on which to focus is the bed. Even if you can't afford the whole bedroom suite, buy the bed you love. The other pieces can be added at a later time, and it isn't necessary for them to match the bed. Cover the bed in good quality bed linens that are soft and inviting. Look for a high thread count and 100-percent Egyptian cotton.

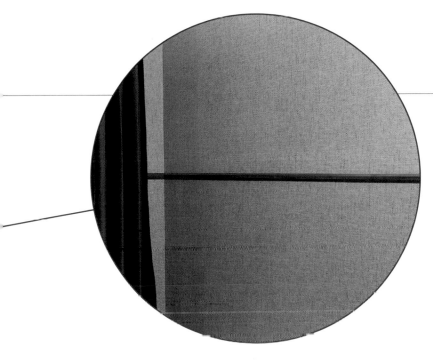

Wall Treatment

The best background to support the outdoor feel inspired by the furniture in this room is a rough texture. The 36-inch-wide woven grass wall covering is a perfect selection. This type of wall covering is traditionally hung vertically. Placing it horizontally, with wood trim to hide the seams, creates a unique background wall treatment.

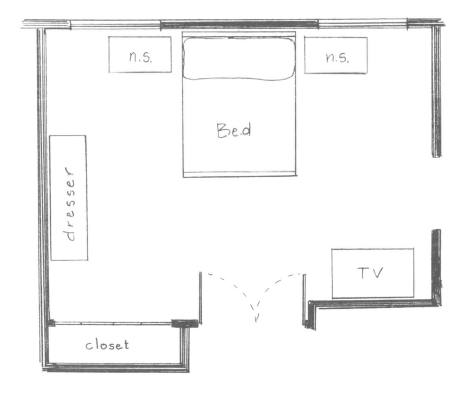

Floor Plan

A good furniture arrangement is one of the keys to success in any room. In a bedroom, start by placing the bed. It should be the first thing you see when you look into the room. Flank the bed with nightstands, and add a storage piece such as a dresser or chest to a wall that is large enough to handle its size. This bedroom is large enough to add an armoire used as an entertainment center. The height of the unit adds some interest and balance to the room.

What's Wrong?

Bare Windows

Windows are wonderful. They bring in the outdoors, light up our spaces and add architectural details. However, they need to be modified for privacy, light control and aesthetics. This usually means adding layers. The windows in this room create too much glare, caused by the contrast between the dark walls and the bright light from outdoors. The brown velvet draperies could be closed, but a better solution is the addition of a sheer or a shade to soften the light.

Bedding

The bedding selected for a bedroom is generally the source of the pattern for the room. Choose a bedspread or duvet cover that pleases your eye and coordinates nicely with the style of furniture you've chosen for the room. It could become the room's inspiration piece and give you all sorts of options for wall colors, drapery colors and accessory ideas. Here, the plaid duvet cover doesn't have enough texture for the room, and the colors are a bit cool for the warmth of the wood furnishings.

Accessories

As with all rooms in your home, the accessories add the finishing touches that complete a beautiful design. When they are overlooked, a room seems cold and without real personality. The master bedroom is the perfect spot for family photos that evoke great memories, fresh flowers that add a lovely scent to the room, or anything else that comforts you.

Let's Get Started!

Inadequate Lighting

Inadequate lighting can mean either the lamp is too small for the space, or the wattage is too low for the task at hand. In this room, the large-scale furniture requires larger fixtures with visual weight. Because the bed is queen size, each nightstand should have a light fixture. A lamp or two on the dresser and a center ceiling fixture are needed for general lighting. This room is large enough for additional accent lighting.

Bare Spaces

A room this size can handle quite a few furniture pieces. Large areas or corners of bare space can make a room look unfinished. Consider what other functions could be served by the addition of a chair and ottoman, additional storage or interesting display space.

Even though this bedroom has lovely furniture, it still has needs. An activities and needs list can uncover special needs that may not be immediately evident to you, especially if you've lived with the room as it is for a long time.

Activities
Watch television

Relaxing

Reading

Needs
Comfy chair

Rocking chair

Good reading light

Inventory
Queen bed

Two nightstands

Armoire

Dresser

Shopping List
Comfy chair: rocker

Lighting: two lamps

Overhead light/fan

New bedding and pillows

Personal accessories

Fixes

Bare Spaces?
Add Furniture!

Bare spaces can give the eyes a rest from busy patterns, but in some rooms, like this master bedroom, the bare spaces give the room an unfinished, empty feeling. It's easy to suggest just adding some furniture, but make sure the additions are appropriate for the room. In other words, they either fulfill one of the functions, create a new function or they are so aesthetically pleasing that they bring joy in just gazing at them!

Rocker

This tooled leather rocking chair is perfect for this room. The leather strapping conforms to the body, giving comfortable support. It rocks—what could be more relaxing? With a built-in leather pouch to hold current magazines, this chair does more than just fill space.

Shelf Unit

This pyramid-shaped accessory shelf is right for several reasons. First, the wood tone is lovely with the rest of the furniture. Second, it adds a tall piece in the opposite corner from the armoire and helps add balance to the room. Third, it offers the ability to display several decorative and even a few functional accessories such as an extra blanket and bird-watching binoculars.

Inadequate Lighting?
Upgrade and Upsize!

Task Lighting

No, the term doesn't sound romantic at all, but task lighting on each nightstand is very important. The lamps must be the correct scale for the furniture. Big furniture means big lamps. Because a queen-size bed is five feet across, two lamps are necessary to provide adequate light to both sides of the bed. This particular style lamp is equipped with a night-light in the curved glass base and a three-way switch, versatile enough to be soft for just relaxing, or brighter for reading and doing crossword puzzles.

Accent Lighting

This bear lamp provides all three types of lighting—general, task and accent. When lit, it provides general light to the room. Since it sits on the dresser, it allows greater visibility in the dresser drawers. It also adds a wonderful outdoor accent to this room.

General Lighting

The true general lighting in this room is provided when the light switch is flipped at the doorway. That switch turns on the light from the fan. This type of lighting is considered general because it doesn't offer quite enough to accomplish tedious tasks, but just enough to get around the room without stubbing toes! The details of this lamp—faux antlers, pinecone brackets and chiseled log motor casing—make this fan/light combination a one-of-a-kind find!

Fixes

Bare Windows?
Add Layers!

The two windows in this room have lovely brown velvet drapes hanging from unique metal rods, which define the windows nicely. To soften the sunlight that streams in through the windows, matchstick blinds are a good choice for filtering the glare. These blinds are light in color, with a brown yarn woven through to create a soft stripe pattern.

Mismatched Bedding?
Update!

The navy blue bedding did not coordinate with the warm wood tones that filled the room. Instead of complementing the furniture, the cool color detracted from it. This primitive patterned duvet does work nicely with the outdoor feel of the furniture and the warm beiges, browns, reds and teals immediately look at home in the room. The single-pleated dust ruffle further softens the look of the bed by hiding some of the wood.

Accessories?
Don't Forget Them!

Add items to the room that are functional as well as decorative. Binoculars and some bird-watching books, a container for snacks, and even a unique moose candleholder are great ways to add color and interest to the space.

Pillows

Matching pillow shams are an excellent way to hide bed pillows that are less than crisp and neat looking. For a different look, consider replacing one or more of them with a plaid Euro sham with rustic detailing. Faux animal skin toss pillows add a rugged touch to this room, and don't you just love the topstitching on the suede pillow?

Special Details

Often, items like switchplate, outlet and vent covers are overlooked when decorating. A cream or white vent cover can be a real eyesore in any room. Shop for covers that coordinate with the backgrounds of your room, like these do.

Projects

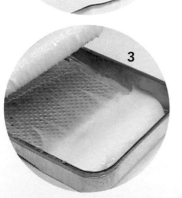

Woven Wall Covering

SHOPPING LIST
Woven wall covering
Heavy-duty wallpaper paste
Wood trim
Stain

MATERIALS ON HAND
Paint roller and tray
Flat-edge blade
Utility knife
Level
Chalk line
Seam roller
Extra utility knife blades

Project note
We applied our wall covering in horizontal bands around the room. The center two strips are the full width of the wall covering, while the top and bottom bands measure approximately 12 inches wide.

1 **Determine the center** of the wall and snap a level chalk line from corner to corner at that point.

2 **Measure the length** of the strip needed. Start flush in a corner and overlap around the next corner by about an inch (photo 1).

3 **Cut wall covering** to length (photo 2) and apply heavy-duty wallpaper paste to the back of the strip using a paint roller (photo 3).

4 **After lining up** the paper with the chalk line, smooth and press the piece into place with your hands. Using your hands instead of a plastic smoother gives you a better feeling for where the bubbles are so that you can correct any issues right away (photo 4). Make sure the edges are adhering around the corner and use a seam roller to make sure the seams are well-adhered.

5 **Wipe off any excess** glue that may have seeped onto the face of the paper.

6 **Repeat Steps 2–5** until the middle two bands of wall covering have been applied to the wall.

7 **When cutting strips** for the top and bottom bands (nearest the crown molding and baseboards), add another inch to the measurement.

8 **Repeat (Steps 2–5)** until the narrow top and bottom bands of the wall are covered. Trim excess paper at the crown molding and baseboards using a flat-edge blade as tight against the edge as possible. The real key to good cuts is in the blade, and when using heavy paper like this, it's a good idea to change the blade after each cut.

9 **Add trim pieces** to cover seams. Cut the trim to the proper length with a miter saw and stain before installing. Nail into place and fill all nail holes with matching wood putty. ■

Hidden Rope Lighting

SHOPPING LIST
Purchased crown molding
2 x 4 lumber
Rope lighting
Rope lighting clips

MATERIALS ON HAND
Table saw
Miter saw
Nail gun or hammer and
    nails
Chalk line
Wood putty

Project note

Because we are attaching crown molding to a room with a vaulted ceiling, there is no place to attach the top of the molding. First we have to attach an angled 2 x 2 cleat to the wall, giving us ample surface area to nail the crown molding in place. The angled cleats are created by cutting a 2 x 4 three times.

1 **Using a table saw,** remove one corner from the long edge of a 2 x 4 with a 45-degree angle.

2 **Turn the 2 x 4** around and remove the other long edge at a 45 degree angle.

3 **Cut the remaining** triangular piece of the 2 x 4 with a straight cut down the center of the board lengthwise, creating two 2 x 2 cleats.

4 **Snap a chalk line** along the wall where the cleats will be attached.

5 **Nail the cleats** to the wall with the wide end toward the ceiling along chalk line.

6 **Attach a rope lighting clip** to the top of each cleat. It's much easier to install the clips at this point than after the crown molding is in place.

7 **Using a miter saw,** cut crown molding to length using 45-degree angles. Remember, for an outside corner, the crown will be longer at the top than at the bottom, and for an inside angle, the crown will be longer at the bottom than at the top. **Note:** *When cutting the crown, imagine that the back of the miter saw is the wall and the horizontal saw plate is the ceiling. Set the molding into position keeping that in mind.*

8 **Nail crown molding** to cleats. A nail gun makes quick work of this.

9 **Fill nail holes** with tinted wood putty.

10 **Install the rope lighting** using the previously installed clips. ■

Project Tip: Have an electrician run a line from the switch up to the connection for the rope lighting so that the lights can be put on a dimmer for the ultimate effect.

Projects

Dried Floral Arrangement

SHOPPING LIST
Container of choice
Floral foam to fit container
As assortment of silk
    sprays, flowers, wheat,
    leaves, seed heads, and
    large and small berries

MATERIALS ON HAND
Scissors
Serrated knife

1 **Place floral foam** in container. Using serrated knife, trim foam so that it is even with the top of the container.

2 **Establish the height** of the arrangement. It should be roughly twice the height of the container. Use the tallest grasses and stems towards the back, with shorter material in front. Let them settle naturally, to establish the width of the display.

3 **Build the density**. Using shorter stems, smaller flowers and seedheads, build up the density in the foreground. Space the stems evenly.

4 **Create focal points** by varying the stem height.

Incorporate larger flowers and seedheads into the display. Place the lowest focal point on an imaginary centerline that runs vertically through the arrangement.

5 **The arrangement** should be balanced from all sides, so inspect it from every angle and adjust as necessary. ■

Duvet Cover

1 Measure width and length of comforter to be covered. Add 1 inch to width and 4½ inches to length; these measurements determine cut dimensions of pieced cover.

2 Cover top: For center panel, cut a panel of one fabric the full width of the fabric times the length determined in Step 1. Cut an identical panel of fabric in half lengthwise for side panels. With right sides facing, align selvage edges with each side of center panel, matching prints. Using a ½-inch seam allowance, sew half panels to full panel. Press seams. Trim side panels evenly so that cover top measures width determined in Step 1.

3 Add cording to right side of cover top, around side and bottom edge.

4 Cover back: Repeat Step 2 with second fabric.

5 Place top and back together, right sides facing. Using a ½-inch seam allowance, sew along side and bottom edges, leaving top edge open.

6 Finish upper edges: Sew upper edges together along side panels only, leaving top edges of center panels open.

7 Cut hook-and-loop tape into three equal pieces; evenly space and adhere tape to open edges, reinforcing them with stitching or permanent fabric adhesive if desired.

8 Hand sew tassels to bottom edge corners.

9 Slide duvet cover over comforter and place on bed. ■

Before

This Master Bedroom

had a great start, with a beautiful bedroom suite, lovely walls and rich draperies. Even so, there was room for improvement. The selection of just the right color and texture for the bedding, along with filling in some of the empty spaces with new pieces of furniture, makes all the difference in this fabulous retreat!

Dens

Sometimes a den, sometimes a home office—an unused bedroom can be as exciting as finding a treasure in your midst. Design it well and it can become one of the busiest rooms in your home.

What's Right?

Multipurpose Furniture

The sleep sofa used in this extra bedroom provides comfortable seating while reading or watching television. If an extra bed is needed, the sofa can be opened to a full-size bed at a moment's notice.

Window Treatment

Metal mini-blinds can be purchased in almost any home store. They are reasonably priced, offer good light control and are a practical first layer for a window treatment.

Before

This Den is typical of in-home work spaces. Crammed into an available corner, they are generally less than attractive areas with poor lighting and organization. **Take it from a pro—a well-designed, functional work environment can raise your self-esteem, boost your confidence and increase your productivity.** Now, in case productivity doesn't go up, at least your surroundings will have improved!

What's Wrong?

Before

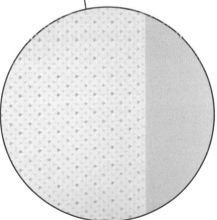

Disproportionate Furniture

Scale is the issue with the current office furniture. The large, four-drawer oak file cabinet overpowers the tiny table used as a desk. The sleep sofa is a good multipurpose piece, but is rarely used as a bed and should be removed from the room.

Backgrounds

A mini floral print wallpaper gives this room little or no personality. Even in a 10 x 12 room, the scale of the pattern is too small.

Furniture Arrangement

This room is large enough to have a better furniture arrangement. Placing upholstered pieces (such as this sofa) in a corner makes the room look smaller than it is and it makes table placement and lighting impossible.

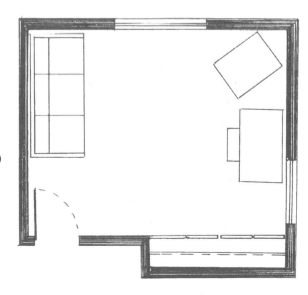

Let's Get Started!

An extra bedroom in a home can be a dream come true. It's your chance to make your home work perfectly for you. Concentrate on the room's function first, before tackling the decor. **Where function is vague, start by creating a list of desired activities. This is the time to be creative and dream big!** Consider unusual activities for which you've never had room, like a gift wrapping area or a place to scrapbook. Once the activities for the room have been decided, address your needs, take inventory and draft a shopping list.

Activities List

Reading

Watching television

Office space

Showing off family photos

Inventory

Computer

Files

Television

Family photos

Needs

Chair/lighting

Television/television stand

Desk (computer and files)

Bookcase or wall space

Framed photos

Shopping List

Comfy chairs

Reading lamps

Television stand

Desk and filing cabinet

Frames

Inspiration

When you've decided on the room's function, it's time to get started with the decorating. There is no better place to begin than with an inspiration piece. In this den, the inspiration is a floral wallcovering and a companion border.

Color, Pattern, Texture

The inspiration wallpaper defines the colors for the room and becomes the dominant pattern. To compliment the floral paper, solid colors and textured fabrics were added in the form of a green leather chair and a tone-on-tone striped chair and ottoman. Don't forget that wood grains add texture to the room as well.

Fixes

Dull Backgrounds?
Add Pattern!

To create a library feel in this room that functions primarily as a woman's space, we selected a floral wallpaper in traditional hues and a coordinating ticking stripe. The ticking stripe didn't add the sophistication we were looking for, and we instead decided to create raised-panel wainscoting all the way around the room. Red paint and glaze on the wainscoting create an aged look which coordinates well with the floral paper above it, making the red tones pop out of the paper.

In this room, we changed the bright white of the ceiling to a soft cream color that matches the background of the wallpaper. Bright white ceilings can look as if they've been forgotten and can seem unattached to the new warmth of a space. Always consider painting the ceiling—it is the fifth wall!

At the ceiling, the coordinating border repeats the bold red of the wainscoting, giving the walls balance. For example, cover the border in the photo. You will see that the upper walls feel light and the lower walls feel heavy. Balance is achieved when you uncover the border.

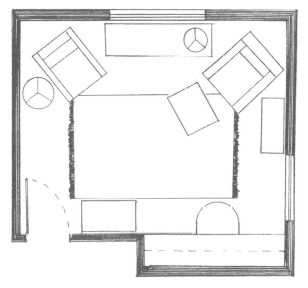

Furniture Arrangement Problems?
Change the Floor Plan!

The decorating details for any room fall into place differently. In this den, the wall color and treatments were chosen first, and then the furniture layout was developed. Thinking outside the box, a brand new functional area is created by simply removing the closet doors. Creating a built-in office area in the former closet space opens up the rest of the room and provides more comfortable seating space for reading and watching television.

Disproportionate Furniture?
Rethink and Replace!

Once the floor plan is finalized, selecting appropriate furniture is easy! Choose chairs for comfort first. A sofa table is a unique way to provide plenty of flat surface space between both chairs without purchasing two tables. A bookcase can either display accessories or hold a collection of books and office supplies.

Fixes

Office Furniture

Using the closet space to create a built-in office is the best decision for this room. Aside from removing the contents of a cluttered closet, this arrangement provides four drawers of filing space, more than ample desktop space and additional upper cabinet storage.

Unappealing Window Treatment?
Get Creative!

Layering at a window is a good way to combine function with an aesthetically pleasing appearance. Consider function first. The goal is privacy and light control without closing off the windows. Wood blinds are the perfect solution! Even with the slats open, they make a great sun shield. When they are closed, there is no way to see into the room. They conveniently pull up out of the way for window cleaning, and the golden wood tone blends in with the floral wallpaper and helps keep the room light. To top off the window, a twist on a traditional pleated valance is attached to the wall above the window with L-brackets, and provides a simple, yet elegant, finishing touch.

Add Personality

Lighting

Replacing the old center ceiling fixture, which is common to most homes, with a small ceiling fan is fairly easy and exceptionally rewarding! Especially in a work atmosphere, a little extra cool air feels refreshing. If the ceiling is high enough or if the fan has a low profile, add a light kit

for general lighting. A set of halogen puck lights installed under the first shelf in the office area provides great task lighting for paperwork or working on the computer. The floor lamp and the lamp on the sofa table are a combination of task and accent lighting.

Accessories
Needn't be Extravagant!

In a room where guests don't frequent, the accessories can be minimal and can even be part of the room's function. For instance, books for pleasure reading are used on the sofa table as accessories—even though they are waiting to be read. Silk plants are fairly inexpensive and they fill a lot of space. Used in combination with some framed family photos and a few collected architectual pieces, the shelf becomes a vital part of the room decor.

Projects

Closet Desk & Storage

SHOPPING LIST

2 wooden two-drawer
   file cabinets

2 ready made upper cabinets

4 x 8 (¾-inch) birch
   plywood

1 x 2 poplar (4 8-foot lenghts)

1 x 12 poplar

Paint and glaze

Clear water-based
   polyurethane

Sheet of plate glass to
   fit desktop (optional)

MATERIALS ON HAND

Table saw or circular saw

Band saw or jigsaw

Hammer and finishing nails

Drill

Wood screws

Nail set

Sandpaper and tack cloth

Tape measure

Painting supplies

Molly bolts

Project Tip: A piece of glass cut to fit the desktop will protect the paint finish from nicks, scratches and coffee stains.

1 **Remove closet doors,** hanging rod and shelving. Patch all holes with spackling compound and prepare walls for painting or papering.

2 **Install ready-made cabinets** inside the closet at eye level. Attach by placing molly bolts through the back of the cabinet into the closet wall.

Add a 1 x 2 support cleat along the back of the closet, flush with the tops of the upper cabinets to support the top shelf. Add a 1 x 2 support cleat along the back of the closet underneath the cabinets to support the lower shelf.

Add a board the width of the closet and the depth of the upper cabinet across the top of the cabinets. Secure with screws.

Cut a board to fit the space between the cabinets, the same depth as the cabinets (or use 1 x 12 poplar board). Attach to the support cleat and cabinet sides with screws.

Install a front fascia board to the bottom of the cabinets and lower shelf.

3 **Place a wooden filing** cabinet at each end of closet inset. Save money by purchasing unfinished cabinets to paint or stain yourself to match existing furniture.

4 **Add a 1 x 2 support cleat** along the back of the closet at the same height as the unfinished file cabinets. This will support the desktop.

5 **Cut a desktop** the width and length of the closet. Use ¾-inch birch plywood for the desktop. Birch paints or stains easily.

6 **Install a front fascia** board to the front of the desktop. Use 1 x 2 poplar for this facing

board. Fill all nail holes with spackling compound and sand all edges smooth.

7 **Paint all cabinets** with a satin latex paint and add a glaze to create an aged effect.

8 **Add several coats** of a water-based satin polyurethane to seal and protect the finish. Add all hardware to the cabinets.

9 **Install puck lighting** underneath the wall cabinets. This can be done by an electrician if you have a fear of electrical projects.

10 **Paint or wallpaper** surrounding walls. ■

Raised-Panel Wainscoting

SHOPPING LIST

1 x 12 poplar lumber

1 x 3 poplar lumber

Flush spackle

Latex satin paint (base
   coat color)

Tea stain glaze

Chair rail

MATERIALS ON HAND

Circular saw

Speed square

Router, router table

Raised panel router bit

Level

Painting supplies

Nail gun & compressor or
   hammer & nails

220-grit sandpaper

Safety gear

1 Establish the wainscoting area in the room. Using a long-level, draw a pencil line around the room at 36 inches from the floor, which will be the location for the top of the chair rail that will be added.

2 Paint the wainscoting area with the base coat color using a brush to cut in and a roller to fill in the larger area. The existing baseboard should also be painted to match the wainscoting. Painting the wall at this point is easier than when the raised panels are added.

3 Using a circular saw, cut the raised panels out of 1 x 12 poplar boards. The panels in the den measured 12 inches wide x 21 inches long. Use a speed square as a cutting guide for the circular saw.

4 Using a router and a router table, rout all the edges of the panels with a raised panel bit. The router table will help keep the routed edge nice and straight. Lightly sand the edges with 220-grit sandpaper. For the den we used a total of 32 panels. This process takes some time. Be patient and be sure to wear safety glasses, hearing protection and a dust mask over your face to avoid inhaling any of the considerable amount of dust produced by the routing process.

5 Prime and paint the panels using a wood primer and the base coat color. *Note: Laying the panels flat on a tarp to paint them is easier than painting them after they have been attached to the wall.*

6 Using a tape measure and level, lay out the location of the panels within the wainscoting area. For this project we measured down six inches from chair rail line and the panels were spaced two inches apart. Make sure the layout is plumb and level.

7 Attach the panels to the wall using construction adhesive on the back and secure in place with one finish nail in each corner. If you have or can rent a nail gun and an air compressor, this will go much faster. Set all the nails with a nail set, and fill the small hole flush with spackling. When dry, touch up with paint.

8 Attach a chair rail to the top of the wainscoting. For the den, we constructed a simple chair rail using two 1 x 3s to create an L-shaped rail. Attach using nails and paint with the base coat color.

9 The entire wainscoting area was antiqued using a tea stain glaze brushed over the base color. Apply with a brush following the direction of the grain of the wood panels. ■

Projects

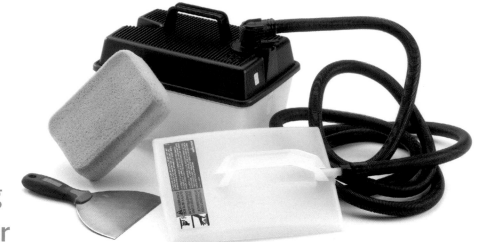

Removing Wall Paper

Project Note

There are several methods for removing wallpaper. Standard ways included liquid removers, gel removers and wallpaper steamers. We have tried them all and prefer using the steamer. It seems to work best, especially when removing several layers of paper.

1 **Before you begin,** protect the flooring by placing drop cloths along the length of the wall. Turn on the steamer so it can heat up.

2 **Score the paper** using a wallpaper scorer (Paper Tiger is a popular name brand). The scorer has small wheels with teeth that perforate the paper, allowing the steam to get behind the paper and loosen the glue. Run the tool over the paper in a circular motion, covering the entire wall.

3 **While you have been doing the prep,** the steamer has been heating up. A word of caution: The steam is hot, so you may want to wear work gloves. Starting at the top of the ceiling, hold the steamer pad tight to the wall, allowing the steam to penetrate. With your other hand, gently remove the paper using a four-inch broad knife. Keep the blade flat to prevent damaging the wall.

4 **Slowly work down** the wall. As you are working, place all of the removed wallpaper into a plastic bag. This will keep the work area neat and it will be easier to move around the room.

5 **After removing the wallpaper,** wash the wall thoroughly with warm water to remove any excess glue. Patch any holes and prime, and then you're ready to paint or paper!

6 **If you choose** to use a liquid remover, just remember to apply the remover and give it enough time to work before trying to scrape off the paper. Remember to read the label for manufacturer's recommendations. ■

Pleated Window Valance

Project note

This lined valance is made of four sections: an upper panel, a lower panel, the pleat flaps and welting. The measurements given in these instructions will fit a window 30 inches wide. To fit your window, specific measuring instructions are given in steps 1 and 2; you will need to adjust cutting measurements.

1 Cut the 1 x 4 board to the width of your window, plus 4 inches (our window measures 30 inches, so we cut the board to 34 inches). Add 8 inches to this measurement to determine the width of the finished valance. Our finished valance measures 42 inches wide.

2 Decide on the length of the valance and divide this measurement into thirds. The top panel of the valance is one-third the width and the bottom panel of the valance is two-thirds the width. Our finished valance measures 18 inches long, with the top panel measuring 6 inches and the bottom panel measuring 12 inches.

3 For the top panel, cut a piece of main fabric measuring 43 inches wide and 7 inches high. For the bottom panel, cut a piece of main fabric measuring 43 inches wide and 13 inches high. Cutting measurements include 1 inch extra for seam allowances.

4 For pleat flaps, cut 5 pieces of main fabric and 5 pieces of coordinating fabric, each measuring 14½ inches wide (top and bottom) and 13 inches high (sides). Place one main color and one contrasting color fabric together with rights sides facing.

Using a ½-inch seam allowance, sew around two sides and bottom, leaving top open. Repeat for remaining pleats. When all pleats are sewn, turn panels right side out and press.

5 To form a pleat, fold each side of panel toward center, with side edges meeting in the center. Folded pleat flap should measure approximately 6¾ inches wide. Repeat for remaining panels to form a total of five pleat flaps.

6 To creating welting, cut a piece of cording 42 inches long. Cut a piece of coordinating fabric 43 inches long and 1½ inch wide. Fold ½ inch of each short end to wrong side and press in place. Place cording along center of wrong side of fabric. Fold fabric around cording and baste in place, using a zipper foot so that stitching is close to cording.

7 To assemble valance front, position raw top edges of pleat flaps along the top of the right side of the lower panel (you'll have 4½ extra inches of the lower panel on either end). Place the raw edge of the welting along the top edge. Place the upper panel on top (with right side facing the right side of the top panel) and sew all four layers together with a ½-inch seam allowance.

8 For lining, cut a piece of coordinating fabric measuring 43 inches wide and 19 inches high. With right sides facing, pin lining to front panel, keeping bottoms of pleat flaps free. Sew panels together using a ½-inch seam allowing, leaving a 6-inch opening along the top edge to turn the valance. Turn valance right side out and press. Turn raw edges of opening under ½ inch and hand sew opening closed.

9 Staple the top of the valance to the 1 x 4 board. Optional: To remove the valance for cleaning, attach it to the board with hook-and-loop tape strips instead of staples. Center board above the window and hang with L-brackets. ∎

Before

This Den has gone through an amazing transformation, both functionally and aesthetically. Office space inset into a closet and comfortable seating create a cozy environment for work, watching television or reading. The best part of the makeover is that the room is now used every single day, which is a wonderful tribute to the importance of decorating!

After

Sunporches

*Free of the confines of solid
interior walls, a sunporch is
a world of its own. It offers
shelter from the elements, and
it combines the best of both
inside and outside. It can easily
become your favorite room in
the house.*

What's Right?

Before

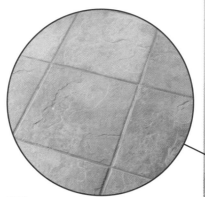

Flooring

A beautiful ceramic tile offers easy maintenance when entering from the outdoors and gives the room a simple elegance that blends nicely with the rest of the home. The tile color coordinates with the interior and exterior colors of the home, blending them for a natural flow between the two.

Ah, the Sunporch! Even in this room's "before" state, it looks like a place you want to be. In other words, some aspects of the room are right. Search for the good in a room first. This starts the decorating process on a positive note. The sunporch has a beautiful view of the outdoors through three walls of sliding glass doors and contains plenty of space to add furniture to expand the room's uses. The overall neutral palette of the walls, floor and ceiling will make decorating a breeze!

The Background Colors

The background colors of this room were somewhat predetermined. The stucco and cedar trim and brick match the exterior decor of the home. The tile flooring gets its personality from mottled hues in the cream of the stucco, the gray of the cedar siding and the warm tones of the adjacent kitchen flooring. Together they create an appropriate outdoor feeling for this three-season room.

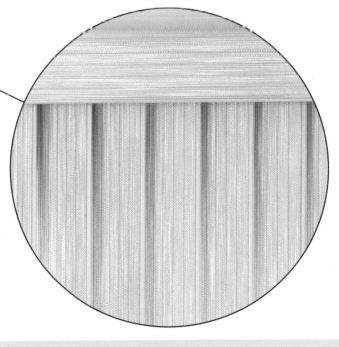

Window Coverings

In this room, three of the walls are really ceiling to floor windows. Therefore, the window treatment decision is just like selecting the wall color. Vertical blinds work well here because they offer privacy and light control. They even stack tightly along the sides of the windows to take advantage of the view. Their string texture, cream color with a touch of gray and a warm neutral, blends with the other neutrals of the background.

What's Wrong?

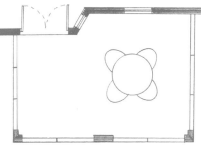

Furniture Arrangement

When we arrived, the sunporch was being used as a hallway to the deck. It contained an outdoor table and chair set, but certainly the full potential of this room wasn't being explored. Measuring 17 feet long and 12 feet wide, the room has ample space for a variety of furnishings.

Before

Accessories

Because this room wasn't being used, accessories were irrelevant. But don't worry—that's going to change!

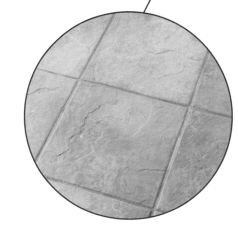

Hard Flooring

Although the tile floor is perfect for this room, it is hard and can feel cold. An area rug placed away from the doors and traffic pattern is a good way to soften the flooring and give the room some warmth.

Let's Get Started!

Creating an activities and needs list is a great way to get started in rooms where specific activities aren't immediately apparent. A Sunporch can sometimes be overlooked as a full-time living space. Plan your activities list to include the same activities you would consider for a living or family room, but with the added advantages of the breeze, the scents and the view of the outdoors. Create a floor plan once you know your needs, then fill in your shopping list!

Furniture

This wire-mesh table and chair set is meant for outdoor use. This room, protected from the outdoor elements, can use softer, more comfortable seating. The room is large enough for a grouping of furniture that can accommodate a multitude of relaxing tasks—from watching television to reading to taking an afternoon nap.

Activities

Reading

Napping

Watching television

Dining for two

Viewing the outdoors

Inventory

No useful furniture

Vertical blinds

Needs

Adequate lighting

Comfortable sofa

Television and stand

Table and chairs

Seating directed toward the outdoors

Shopping

Chairs and sofa

Side table and lamps

Television and stand

Small bistro table and two chairs

Fixes

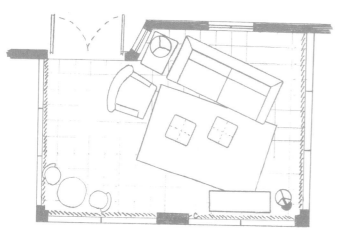

Furniture Arrangement Problems?
Draw a Floor Plan!

Placing the sofa at an angle to face the windows helps take advantage of the wonderful view of the backyard. Once the sofa is in place, arranging the chair, side table and television cabinet is easy. A bistro table and two chairs fill in the empty corner and provide a cozy place for an intimate dinner for two.

No Usable Furniture?
Shop the Sales!

The sofa is a transitional style that has fairly clean, contemporary lines, but the soft curved arms and turned legs are more traditional. The plaid fabric, which is in a contemporary color combination, is a slipcover, so it can be cleaned or changed in the future to give the room an entirely new look. It's the perfect place for an afternoon nap.

The rocker is covered in a gray denim that works nicely with the neutrals in the space. The soft curved arms and plump cushion are inviting and casual. What a great place to sit and read!

For optimal TV viewing, place the screen so it faces away from the outside windows to eliminate glare. Since the back of the credenza will be placed along the window, make sure it is finished because the back will be visible from the outside. Small details like this make a room seem planned and not just happenstance.

Who could resist this slate-top bistro set? It was exactly what was needed to enjoy breakfast or an evening snack. The corner of the sunporch has become a convenient and relaxing area for working on crossword puzzles or playing a game with the kids.

Hard Flooring? **Add a Rug!**

To soften the hard surface of the tiled floor, the addition of a 5 x 7 area rug placed within the sofa and chair grouping not only adds softness but also warmth on chilly mornings or brisk fall days. For this room, we introduced a contemporary rug with fun geometric patterns in a variety of colors that you may not expect. The oranges and golds add life to the space and the rug becomes a fabulous focal point.

No Accessories? **Buy or Make Your Own!**

Because this sunporch leans toward a contemporary style, the addition of accessories is kept to a minimum. Pillows add a splash of color on the sofa and are comfortable for afternoon napping. Glass vases that match the sofa add interest to an outside corner of the room. The TV cabinet is a convenient area to place books for quiet reading and a clock to keep track of your favorite television show!

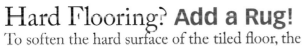

Lighting

Even in a room with lots of natural light streaming in, lighting is critical. Evenings in this sunporch are a perfect time to unwind from a hard day of work or play. For reading, task lighting is required. A table lamp on the side table fits the bill nicely. Make sure when you are seated you cannot see the bare bulb. Lamps with three-way switches allow different settings, low for conversation or high for reading.

Accent lighting for the corner is accomplished with this contemporary accordion lamp. When plugged into a dimmer cord, it becomes a soft light for television viewing.

Place a pendant light fixture above the informal dining area to provide ample light for eating and playing games. The wrought iron coordinates well with the painted furniture, and the floral design blends nicely with the view of the outdoors. When all three lamps are used together, they provide all the general lighting this room requires.

Add Personality

Ceiling Fan

A ceiling fan is a welcome fixture to provide a cool breeze on warm days. The wicker blades of the fan blend nicely with the rough background textures in this room.

TV Set

Matt thinks every room needs its own television and this homeowner feels the same way. Fortunately, with flat-screen televisions becoming smaller and smaller, the television doesn't need to be the focal point of the room. Instead, it can be placed in an unobtrusive location for convenient viewing.

Draperies

A window on the interior wall leading into the kitchen of the home has been softened by a patterned throw turned into an informal drape. The wrought-iron rod echoes the light fixtures and black furniture.

Table Setting

Keeping place mats and napkins on the table isn't necessary, but they certainly soften the hard tile surface. The colors of the napkins and mats are drawn directly from the area rug, pulling a spark of bright color to the corner. Remember, it's the little details that make the biggest impression.

Projects

Ceiling Grid

SHOPPING LIST
½-inch wood trim
Paint

MATERIALS ON HAND
Miter saw
Nail gun or hammer and
  nails
Table saw
Pencil
Straightedge
Wood putty
Two sawhorses

Project note

This grid does a great job of hiding unsightly and uneven ceiling lines—perfect for sunporches where ceilings are usually constructed with sheets of 4 x 8 plywood.

1 **Use a pencil and straightedge** to draw an overall 2 x 2-foot grid directly on the ceiling as a guide to lay out the wood trim (photo 1).

2 **Paint the trim** before cutting and installing. Lay out the pieces on sawhorses and roll on the paint. It's much easier than painting when it's on the ceiling (photo 2).

3 **Use a miter saw** to cut trim pieces into 2-foot lengths. Make two 45-degree angle cuts in

the center of each end. The end will resemble an arrow tip (photo 3).

4 **Use a nail gun to nail trim** into position along the layout lines (photo 4). The painted trim piece should be lined up with the grid corner.

5 **For all perimeter trim,** rip pieces down the middle using a table saw. This trim should only be half the width of the grid trim and should be placed along all outside edges to finish the ceiling. ■

Beaded Pillows

SHOPPING LIST
Fabric of choice
Pillow form
Prestrung beads
Thread to match fabric

MATERIALS ON HAND
Sewing needle
Scissors
Measuring tape

1 **Measure length and width** of pillow form and cut a front panel.

2 **Cut a second panel** the same width but 4 inches longer. Then cut this panel in half across the width. This creates two pieces that will overlap in the center for the back panel.

3 **Sew a ½-inch hem** along the edge just cut on the two back panels. When they are hemmed, overlap them to match

the size of the front panel. Pin overlap in place.

4 **Measure perimeter** of front panel using measuring tape.

5 **Cut a length** of decorative beads to the pillow perimeter measurement, adding 1 inch.

6 **Pin decorative beads** along the perimeter of the front panel with the beads to the inside and the beading ribbon along the edge.

7 **With right sides facing,** pin the back panel to the front panel. Sew around the perimeter, sandwiching the bead ribbon between the two layers.

8 **Remove all pins,** including those holding the overlap together, and turn the beaded pillow cover right side out.

9 **Slip the cover** over the pillow form and enjoy! ∎

Projects

Create Your Own Art

SHOPPING LIST
Foam brushes
Purchased multiwindow
mat and frame
Acrylic paint
Watercolor paper

1 Using foam brushes and acrylic paint, randomly paint abstract shapes such as blocks, lines and circles to completely fill the watercolor paper. Allow paint to dry between colors.

2 When the paint is dry, splatter or drip black acrylic paint over them. Allow the paint to dry completely.

3 Tape artwork to the back of the mat, then frame and hang. ■

Tile Floor

SHOPPING LIST
Ceramic tile
Quick-set mortar
Grout mix
Rubber grout float
Grout sponge
Plastic tile spacers
½-inch notched trowel
Tile cutter

MATERIALS ON HAND
Needle-nose pliers

1 **Start by deciding on the layout.** Consider where you want to see full, uncut tiles. Lay them out to find the center of the room. Draw reference lines to locate the center starting point.

2 **Mix a batch** of quick-set mortar according to manufacturer's instructions. Using a ½-inch notched trowel, spread mortar evenly along reference line, creating furrows in the mortar bed (photo 1).

3 **Set the first tile** in the corner along the lines, and twist the tile as you place it in position (photo 2). Then, gently tap it in the center with the palm of your hand to set it evenly in the mortar.

4 **Use temporary plastic** tile spacers at the corners of the set tiles to ensure even spacing (photo 3). Remove them with needle-nose pliers before the mortar hardens.

5 **Following manufacturer's directions,** use a tile cutter to cut partial tiles as needed (photo 4). Apply mortar to back of cut tiles and slip them into place along the wall.

6 **Let mortar cure** for 24 hours.

7 **Mix grout** according to manufacturer's directions. Starting in a corner, scoop some grout onto the tile. Using a rubber grout float, spread the grout out from the corner, pressing firmly on the float to completely fill the joints. A figure-eight motion works well for this. Then wiping diagonally across the joints, use the float to remove the excess grout (photo 5).

8 **After about a 5-foot** square area is grouted, use a damp grout sponge to remove even more of the excess grout (photo 6). Work in a small area and wipe each area only once, rinsing the sponge with cool water between wipes. This is probably the most time-consuming task of the whole job.

9 **Let the grout dry** for about four hours, then flip the sponge over and use the abrasive side on the tile surface to remove any remaining grout. ■

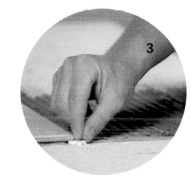

Before

After

This Sunporch has now become a functional, comfortable addition to the home. In fact, it's a destination instead of just a hallway to the backyard. The neutral colors are calming and restful, and when they're accented with a bold palette of color as in the area rug, the room really comes to life.

Matt & Shari's
Shopping List & Resources

Page 28 Entryways
Paint: walls: Rye Grass SW6423; cabinet and
    shelves: Tricorn Black SW6258 (Sherwin-Williams)
Trim paint: #930 (Benjamin Moore Paints)
Cabinet accessories: black leather boxes, tall
    dog statue, velvet scarf (Marshalls)
Round table accessories: dalmatian glass, white
    square plate, white bowl (T.J. Maxx)
Unfinished two-door cabinet: model #9020
    (Colors of Wood)
Pendant light fixture (Lowe's Companies Inc.)
Wall hanging and hanging vase
    (Houseworks Inc.)
Ochre candles, black vase (Cost Plus World Market)

Page 46 Great Rooms
Paint: accent wall: Leather Bound SW6118
    (Sherwin-Williams)
Window shades: Provenance Woven Wood
    blinds, Mindanao, WWMN468 (Hunter Douglas
    Window Fashions)
Wall accessories: mounted plates, pineapple
    candles, bowls on coffee table (Yankee Barn)
Pillows (Burlington Coat Factory)
Topiaries (Jo-Ann Etc.)
Trapunto Quilt, P44340 full/queen (Plow & Hearth
    Home catalog)

Page 62 Dining Rooms
Wall art, buffet lamps and chandelier shades
    (Bed Bath & Beyond)
Tall glass vases (Pier 1 Imports)
Small accessories on wine rack (T.J. Maxx)
Wine racks (Cost Plus World Market)

Page 80 Kitchens
Ceiling paint: Water Chestnut SW1136 (Sherwin-
    Williams)
Wallpaper: #AV2166, stripes, #AV4014, village
    scenes (Imperial)

Page 96 Bathrooms
Paint: topcoat of washing technique: Lingering
    Blue SW1513 (Sherwin-Williams) stamped
    leaf colors: Lingering Blue SW1513, Spa Blue
    SW1498, Uphill SW1428 (Sherwin-Williams)
Window pocket sheers (Pottery Barn)
Towels (Bed, Bath & Beyond)
Countertop cubbyhole shelf (Pier 1 Imports)
Area rugs (Lowe's Companies Inc.)

Page 112 Children's Rooms
Paint pens, large wooden letters (Jo-Ann Etc.)
2-inch wooden blinds: Country Woods (Hunter
    Douglas Window Fashions)
Drapes, small wooden stools, solid-colored
    pillows (Bed, Bath & Beyond)
Bedding (The Land of Nod)
Blanket for Little Brave bed (Pendleton)
Stagecoach lamp (Levin Furniture)
Galloping ponies for clothes hooks (Toys R Us)
Square bean bag ottomans (Target
    Department Store)

Page 128 Teen Rooms
Paint: Serenity SW1494 (Sherwin-Williams)
Sheets and comforter cover (Bed, Bath &
    Beyond)
Accessory pillows (Bed, Bath & Beyond)
Bedroom furniture (Ethan Allen Home Interiors)
Lamps (Target Department Store)
Area rug (Pottery Barn)
Lavender glass garland (T.J. Maxx)
White desk and chair (Pier 1 Imports)

Page 144 Master Bedrooms
Bedroom furniture, metal bear lamps, leather
    rocker, stag picture (Levin Furniture)
Faux antler ceiling fan (The Horchow Collection)
Nightstand lamps, bedding, faux fur throw,
    brown velvet drapes, drapery hardware,
    throw on pyramid shelves (Bed, Bath &
    Beyond)
Pyramid-shaped shelving unit, boxes on
    dresser (Cost Plus World Market)
"The Buck Stops Here" pillow (T.J. Maxx)

Page 160 Dens
Red base coat paint: Hot Apple Spice #2005-20
    (Benjamin Moore)
Glaze: Tea Stain #AG02 (Ralph Lauren)
Wallpaper (Imperial)
Beige trim paint: Croissant #SW1114 (Sherwin-
    Williams)
Ceiling paint: Irish Cream #SW1115 (Sherwin-
    Williams)
Area rug: Ancient Inspirations #DO96C44,
    Kirman light green (Waxman's Carpet and
    Rug Warehouse)
Oak bookshelf: Peters-Revington Co., model
    #26560 (Basista Furniture)

TV stand: #2312, sofa table: #2315 (Wayside
    Furniture)
Armchair: #1107, ottoman: #11070 Pembrook in
    Cuzco Linen (Levin Furniture)
Ceiling fan: Hunter (Lowe's Companies Inc.)
Lamps (Pottery Barn)

Page 176 Sunporches
Slate-topped table, bistro chairs, accent pillows
    (Pier 1 Imports)

Floor lantern, paisley throw blankets, aqua
    vases (Cost Plus World Market)
Window coverings: taupe Innerstyle with
    louver groover Allure (Hunter Douglas)
Sofa, rocker, console table, side table (Sofa
    Express)
Area rug (Waxman's Carpet and Rug Warehouse)
Table lamp (Target Department Store)
Black leather ottomans (Bed, Bath & Beyond)

Carpet
Waxman's Carpet and Rug Warehouse
Phone: (440) 734-7060

Decorative Project Materials
Bed Bath & Beyond
Toll-free: 800-462-3966
Fax: (973) 785-4255
E-mail: customer.service@bedbath.com
Web site: www.bedbathandbeyond.com

Burlington Coat Factory
Toll-free: (800) 446-2628
Web site: www.coats.com

Cost Plus World Market
Phone: (310) 441-5115
Web site: www.costplus.com

The Horchow Collection
Phone: (972) 556-6000
Toll Free Phone: (800) 825-8000
Web site: www.horchow.com

Houseworks Inc.
Phone: (216) 378-3463

Jo-Ann Fabrics & Crafts / Jo-Ann Etc.
Phone: (330) 656-2600
Toll-free: (888) 739-4120
Fax: (330) 463-6670
Web site: www.joann.com

The Land of Nod
Toll-Free Phone: (800) 933-9904
Web site: www.landofnod.com

Lowe's Companies, Inc.
Toll-free: (800) 445-6937
Web site: www.lowes.com

Marshalls
Phone: (508) 390-3000
Toll-free: (888) 627-7425
Fax: (508) 390-2366
Web site: www.marshallonline.com

Pendleton
Web site: www.pendleton-use.com

Pier 1 Imports
Toll-Free: (800) 245-4595
Web site: www.pier1.com

Plow & Hearth Home Catalog
Toll-free: (800) 494-7544
Web site: www.plowhearth.com

Pottery Barn
Toll-free: (888) 779-5176
Web site: www.potterybarn.com

T.J. Maxx
Toll-free: (800) 926-6299
Web site: www.tjx.com

Target Department Store
Toll-free: (800) 800-8800
Web site: www.target.com

Toys R Us
Web site: www.toysrus.com

Yankee Barn
Phone: (330) 877-6507

Furniture
Basista Furniture
Phone: (216) 398-5900

Ethan Allen Home Interiors
26127 Lorain Road
North Olmsted, OH 44070

Levin Furniture
Phone: (440) 716-2200

Sofa Express
1739 Brittain Rd.
Akron, OH 44310
Phone: (330) 630-1399

Wayside Furniture
1367 Canton Rd.
Cleveland, OH 44102
Phone: (216) 691-1699

Paint
Benjamin Moore Paints
Toll-free: (888) 236-6667
Web site: www.benjaminmoore.com

Ralph Lauren
Glidden Company
Toll-free: (800) 454-3336
Web site: www.gliddenpaints.com

Sherwin-Williams
The Sherwin-Williams Company
Toll-free: (800) 474-3794
Web site: www.sherwin-williams.com

Unfinished Furniture
Colors of Wood
Phone: (440) 842-4451

Wallpaper
Blue Mountain Wallcoverings Inc.
Phone: (216) 464-3700
Toll-free Phone: (800) 539-5399
Web site: www.ihdg.com

Window Coverings
Hunter Douglas Window Fashions
Phone: (303) 466-1848
Toll-free: (800) 937-7895
E-mail: consumer@hunterdouglas.com
Web site: www.hunterdouglas.com